THORA HIRD'S
PRAISE BE! NOTEBOOK

Elizabeth Gort has worked with Thora on Praise
Be! for fourteen years, first as a BBC Television
producer, and, for the past three years, as an
independent writer and broadcaster.

They share the same birthday and have become
close friends.

For Dear, Dear
Katt

Freda ;

D0892590

THORA HIRD'S

Praise Be!

NOTEBOOK

**Thora Hird
and Elizabeth Gort**

Collins
FOUNT PAPERBACKS

First published in Great Britain 1990 by
Fount Paperbacks
Fourth reprint November 1990
Fount Paperbacks is an imprint of the
Collins Religious Division
part of the HarperCollins Publishing Group
77–85 Fulham Palace Road, London W6 8JB

Copyright © 1990 Thora Hird and Elizabeth Gort

Typeset by Avocet Robinson, Buckingham
Printed and bound in Great Britain by
Cox & Wyman Ltd, Reading

Conditions of Sale

This book is sold subject to the condition
that it shall not, by way of trade or otherwise,
be lent, re-sold, hired out or otherwise circulated
without the publisher's prior consent in any form of
binding or cover other than that in which it is
published and without a similar condition
including this condition being imposed
upon the subsequent purchaser.

This book is dedicated to the viewers of *Praise Be!*,
Whose faithfulness for thirteen years has meant so
  much to me.
We are now in the fourteenth year of hymns that you
  request;
To bring in all the hymns you choose I try my very
  best.
To those of you I disappoint, I'm sorry — that's quite
  true.
So I've compiled this little book especially for you.

ACKNOWLEDGEMENTS

We are grateful to the following for permission to reprint their work: Revd Mother Pamela CAH for *Easter* by Sr Maud CAH, Hope Publishing Co., Carol Stream, Illinois, for *Great is Thy Faithfulness* by T O Chisolm and *You Shall Go Out With Joy* by S Dauermann, Thankyou Music, PO Box 75, Eastbourne, East Sussex, for *How Great Thou Art*, trans. by Stuart K Hine, David Higham Associates for *Morning has Broken* by Eleanor Farjeon, Robert L Bell, Melrose, Massachussetts, for *Desiderata* by Max Ehrmann, Stainer & Bell Ltd, PO Box 110, 82 High Rd, London, for *When I Needed a Neighbour* by Sidney Carter, Franciscan Communications Centre, 1229 S Sante St, Los Angeles, California 90015, for *Make Me a Channel of Your Peace*, George Bennard, The Rodeheaver Company, Northridge Rd, Berkhamsted, Herts, for *The Old Rugged Cross*, Clemency Greatorex for *Martha's Prayer*, The Chaplain, Royal Chelsea Hospital, for *Nursing the Elderly* by Kathy Doyle, ofr *This is the Day*, Oxford University Press, Walton St, Oxford, OX2 6DP, for *Ye Choirs of New Jerusalem*, trans. by R Campbell.

Every effort has been made to trace the copyright owners of material included in this book. However, the publishers would be grateful if any omission in these acknowledgements could be brought to their attention, for correction in future editions.

CONTENTS

INTRODUCTION

I've been presenting **Praise Be!** for fourteen years now, and it's been one of the great pleasures of my life – I hardly think of it as work, although as a matter of fact, a very great deal of work does go into it.

One thing I like to do each year is to make notes of anything that catches my eye, so I can remember to mention it. Many's the time Jimmy and I have been driving along in the car and I've said to him "Stop! Oh Stop!" and he always says "Oh Thor! What is it now?" (He loves me really, but if I could have a pound for every time he's said "Oh Thor!" . . .) It might be a row of brownies cleaning out a hedge, which we saw one year – twelve little bottoms all sticking up in a row. Or a Salvation Army Band. And I love those notices you see outside churches – Wayside Pulpits, I think they call them. Whenever I see a good one, I make him stop so I can write it down.

The greatest joy has been receiving all the letters from viewers, telling me their stories and about the hymns they love. It's these letters which literally make the programmes happen. They select the hymns, and the stories they tell provide much of the inspiration for **Praise Be!** There are so many wonderful, brave people in the world, who nobody ever hears about. I want to dedicate this book to them.

This book is a collection – from A to Z – of some of their and my favourite hymns, and of some of the thoughts and ideas that have gone into making **Praise**

Be! over the years. It's about hymns, about people, about faith. I hope you like it.

THORA HIRD

At the Gate of the Year

And I said to the man who stood at the gate of the year:
"Give me a light that I may tread safely into the unknown."
And he replied:
"Go out into the darkness and put your hand into the hand of God. That shall be to you better than light and safer than a known way."

from *God Knows* by Louise Haskins – The Gate of the Year

All Things Bright and Beautiful

Since I first started presenting hymns on **Praise Be!** in 1976 – or **Your Songs of Praise Choice** as it was then called (Crikee! What a tongue-twister that was! I once entertained the crew for nearly a quarter of an hour, demonstrating all the different ways you could say it . . . I think that was when the Producer decided to change the name to **Praise Be!**) – but as I was saying before I interrupted myself, since those far off days hymn fashions have changed, and some of the most popular ones today are hymns that I'd never even heard of when we started.

For instance, how long have you been singing "Make Me a Channel of Your Peace" in your church? It's a beautiful little folkhymn based on the prayer of St Francis, but it's only quite recently that most of us have come to know it; and then there's "Our God Reigns", a rousing hymn that the one-million-strong crowds sang at those vast open air masses during Pope John Paul 2's visit to Britain in 1982, and have gone on requesting ever since. Even more recently, just in the last year or two, I've been inundated with requests for hymns composed and written by a prolific young hymn-writer called Graham Kendrick.

There's one hymn, though, that I have included every year from the beginning, and I'm certain that as long as people are writing in to ask for their favourite hymns, it will always be among them – "All Things Bright and Beautiful", written for children by Mrs Alexander in 1884, to illustrate the words of the Creed: "Maker of Heaven and Earth". The hymn is usually sung on **Songs of Praise** several times each year, and I always look out for one where there's a choir of children leading the singing.

That's been one of the greatest pleasures of working on **Praise Be!** for me, seeing all the little children singing so earnestly. The camera pans along a row of faces, and you wonder what life has in store for them. Sometimes I think I can see a future actress among them, putting all she's got into it, bless her, or a boy who is definitely going to be for it when his mother sees him on television, nudging his neighbour, his hair on end and tie askew. He'd probably been tidied up only minutes before they went "on air", too.

I hope they don't forget this time in their lives, when they stood huddled together in a church, or cathedral, or sometimes out in the open air looking very wind-blown, and because of television, millions of people saw and heard them singing "All things bright and beautiful" and thought "Aaah!"

All things bright and beautiful
All creatures great and small
All things wise and wonderful
The Lord God made them all.

Each little flower that opens
Each little bird that sings
He made their glowing colours,
He made their tiny wings:

The purple-headed mountain,
The river running by,
The sunset and the morning
That brightens up the sky:

The cold wind in the winter,
The pleasant summer sun,
The ripe fruits in the garden
He made them every one:

He gave us eyes to see them,
And lips that we might tell
How great is God Almighty,
who has made all things well:

All things bright and beautiful
All creatures great and small
All things wise and wonderful
The Lord God made them all.

Mrs Cecil Frances Alexander
(1818–1895)

Acting

I enjoy being an actress, and I hope I never have to stop. Sometimes people ask me why I don't take things easier now, do less. My answer is "Why? Do you want me to die?" That may sound odd to you, but the Lord has been very good to me in this particular way: when I'm working, I never have any pain. When I stop, that's when I remember that A is for Angina and Arthritis and Aching Artificial hips . . .!

I made my first stage appearance at the age of eight weeks in a play directed by my father. I played "the unfortunate result" of the young heroine, played by my mother, having been seduced by the Squire's son. While this important role did not immediately lead to the offer of other parts, we lived next door to the Royalty Theatre, Morecambe, at number 6 Cheapside, so my brother Neville and I spent much of our childhood in and around the theatre, and from as long ago as I can remember, my dream was to be an actress when I grew up.

Although they had hoped I might settle for a less perilous career, when I was offered my first professional role (which was very tiny) in repertory, I had the support, help, encouragement and criticism of two of the cleverest, most professional people you could find anywhere in the world, my mother and father. How many actresses, starting out, pop out from their dressing room and within a count of twenty are able to be in their own living-room, asking their very experienced and professional mother, "How do I look, I've not overdone it, have I?"

I've written all about those happy early days in Morecambe in my autobiography, *Scene and Hird*, and they've remained fresh in my mind. Jimmy and I still spend many a happy evening saying to one another, "Do you remember. . . .?" because they were, they really were, as I so often say, happy days.

So much of what I cherish about my childhood is to do with the kindness and love of the folk I grew up with, and the rhythms and rituals of everyday life in those days, in a part of England where people were always neighbourly – loving, helpful, nosy, irritating, funny. When viewers, particularly the older ones, write to me now on **Praise Be!** about their own memories and stories, I find that they so often chime in with mine, and it all comes back.

Am I acting when I present **Praise Be!**? Well, yes, I am in a way. I truly mean and believe all the things I say on the programme, but, for instance, **Praise Be!** isn't "live", so that when I say something like: "Lizzie Mint? Are you watching? This next hymn's for you!' I know Lizzie Mint isn't really watching when I say it, and won't be until the programme is shown on television a few days or weeks later. When it does go out on the air, as often as not it isn't only Lizzie Mint who (we hope) is watching, but Scotty and I, too, are sitting at home watching **Praise Be!** And I'm here to tell you, it's a funny feeling sitting at home by our television set watching me sitting at home by our television set!

So, I do have to make believe, when I talk to the viewers, that they are there listening to me, and I suppose you could call that acting . . . But as with all acting, when I'm doing it, I believe in it, and the viewers themselves, by writing me their loving letters, help me to know that I'm talking to friends – and they do eventually hear me!

A hymn that I've always felt unites us all in its beautiful
poetry about common experiences and feelings is "Abide
with Me."

Abide With Me

Abide with me; fast falls the eventide;
The darkness deepens; Lord, with me abide;
When other helpers fail, and comforts flee,
Help of the helpless, O, abide with me.

Swift to its close ebbs out life's little day;
Earth's joys grow dim, its glories pass away;
Change and decay in all around I see;
O Thou, who changest not, abide with me.

I fear no foe with Thee at hand to bless;
Ills have no weight, and tears no bitterness;
Where is death's sting? Where, Grave, thy victory?
I triumph still, if Thou abide with me.

Hold Thou Thy Cross before my closing eyes;
Shine through the gloom, and point me to the skies;
Heaven's morning breaks, and earth's vain shadows flee;
In life, in death, O Lord, abide with me.

H. Francis Lyte (1793–1847)

This is a BaPtist church
Be Part of it!

(Do you remember the BP sale advertisements?)

Beatitudes

And seeing the multitudes, He went up into a mountain: and when He was set, His disciples came unto Him: And He opened His mouth, and taught them, saying, Blessed are the poor in spirit: for theirs is the kingdom of heaven.

Blessed are they that mourn: for they shall be comforted.

Blessed are the meek: for they shall inherit the earth.

Blessed are they which do hunger and thirst after righteousness: for they shall be filled.

Blessed are the merciful: for they shall obtain mercy.

Blessed are the pure in heart: for they shall see God.

Blessed are the peace-makers: for they shall be called the children of God.

Blessed are they which are persecuted for righteousness' sake: for theirs is the kingdom of heaven.

Blessed are ye, when men shall revile you, and persecute you, and shall say all manner of evil against you falsely, for My sake.

Rejoice, and be exceeding glad: for great is your reward in heaven.

St Matthew Chapter 4 (AV)

Bible

I always try to include at least one Bible reading in each series of **Praise Be!**, like the beautiful passage I've just quoted, Jesus' own words from the Sermon on the Mount. Some people seem to be a bit frightened of the Bible, and think it's going to be very difficult to understand, or boring, or that it's something only the vicar should read. Well, I'm no clever head, but I don't see it like that at all. To me it's a book full of marvellous stories about ordinary people to whom extraordinary things happen.

Both the Old and New Testaments are full of tales of men and women who are completely changed when they discover God in their lives – especially when you think of some of the stories Jesus himself told, like the one about the Prodigal Son, and the Good Samaritan. Now, I may be wrong, but I think it's possible that an ordinary, down to earth actress, like myself, can sometimes put these stories across better than someone who tries to read them in a very solemn, holy sort of a voice. And believe me, there are no better words for an actress to read.

I'd never want to preach on **Praise Be!** and I couldn't if I wanted to. I know nothing about theology, I leave all that to the vicar. What being a Christian means to me is having the Lord as a friend, who I can talk to. Oh yes, I'm always having little chats with Him. That's what makes all the difference in my life, and it helps me understand all those other ordinary men and women in the Bible. But please don't ask me to explain the doctrine of the Trinity to you, or tell you how many angels can balance on the point of a pin.

I have so many blessings to thank the Lord for, and one of the best things in the last few years has been having my daughter, Jan (Janette Scott), back home in England after so many years in America. She's always near by when we record **Praise Be!** at her home in Sussex, where Jimmy and I have our dear little cottage in her garden. So sometimes she joins me on the programme, and she, too, reads passages from the Bible in her beautiful voice, which I know gives great pleasure.

By the way, I think you would be surprised to see how many people there are in the room with me when we're recording **Praise Be!** Apart from Jan and me, and – sometimes – Scotty sitting near by (when he hasn't nipped out to do a bit of gardening. You sometimes see him walking past the window behind me when he's had enough!), there's the producer, the director, the assistant producer, the engineer, the electrician, the cameraman, the assistant cameraman, the sound recordist, the make-up artist, and an autocue operator (reminding me of everyone's names, and what hymn is coming up next). Go on! You must think I'm a marvel if you think I could remember it all!

This next hymn is based on the Beatitudes. Sometimes it's easier to remember the words of hymns than words in the Bible. I call hymns the Church's folk music!

Blest are the Pure in Heart

Blest are the pure in heart,
For they shall see our God,
The secret of the Lord is theirs,
Their soul is Christ's abode.

The Lord, who left the heavens
Our life and peace to bring,
To dwell in lowliness with men,
their Pattern and their King;

Still to the lowly soul
He doth Himself impart,
And for His dwelling and His throne
Chooseth the pure in heart.

Lord, we Thy presence seek;
May ours this blessing be;
give us a pure and lowly heart
A temple meet for Thee.

J. Keble (1792–1866)

Bells

I don't want you to think I'm boasting, but church bells
were rung the day I was born. Well, it was a Sunday
morning!

PS: Blessed are those who can laugh at themselves; they
will have endless amusement!

Count Your Blessings

When upon life's billows you are tempest toss'd,
Are you ever burden'd with a load of care?
When you look at others with their lands and gold,
So amid the conflict, whether great or small,

Count your many blessings, name them one by one,
Count your many blessings, ev'ry doubt will fly,
Count your many blessings, money cannot buy
Count your many blessings, angels will attend,

When you are discourag'd, thinking all is lost,
Does the cross seem heavy you are call'd to bear?
Think that Christ has promis'd you His wealth untold,
Do not be discourag'd, God is over all,

And it will surprise you what the Lord hath done.
And you will be singing as the days go by.
Your reward in heaven, nor your home on high.
Help and comfort give you to your journey's end.

Count Your Blessings

If **Praise Be!** had the equivalent of a school motto, "Count your blessings" would be it. I get so many letters from people with terrible troubles, handicaps, pain, loneliness, people who are very ill themselves, or who have nursed someone they love through great illness. Yet very rare indeed is the letter that contains even a scrap of self-pity. They write to tell me how this or that thing has helped them. Sometimes, and I feel very blessed that this should be so, they tell me that they have been watching **Praise Be!** and I have played some hymn that has lifted them out of a moment of near despair. I think great hymns well sung make us all feel better.

Dear Thora,
Last Sunday I watched **Praise Be!** and was wonderfully comforted by the hymn ''Be not Afraid''.

It was very appropriate as I was due to enter Wythenshawe Hospital on the following day for an operation, and was very frightened of the outcome.

I am now recovering from the op., but felt compelled to tell you what I went in with a little more courage after watching your programme.
God bless you.
Winifred A. Shaw (Mrs)
Ashton-u-Lyne

Dear Thora,
I write on behalf of my 97-year-old Mother, who has been bedbound in my house since November 1986. **Songs of Praise** and **Praise Be!** are the highlights of our week. Mother cannot see the TV and cannot really hear, but I sing loudly in her ear, and there are many hymns she knows and sings. This, with our curate bringing communion to us weekly, keeps our ''Churchgoing'' regular and gives us both great enjoyment.

So I would like to thank you very much indeed for your programme. You and "sport" are really all we watch! My Mother and I both played hockey for England and she was a super tennis coach, so you can understand why.

Yours sincerely,
Mary Eyre
Cheltenham

Dear Thora,

. . . I am 86 on 2nd September (D.V.) and though lively and fairly active, especially in my church work and photography, I've already asked for that hymn "How Great Thou Art" to be sung at my Memorial service, and told them, if I still have a voice in the Life Beyond, I'll join in and sing with them!'

I'm not being morbid. I've had a good life, a good husband (who died at 85, two years ago), a good family, and sincere faith. In April I visited my granddaughters in San Diego and Kansas City, and last October was on ITV in "Living it up". So I'm not morbid, am I?

But, being very deaf, I enjoy your programmes because I can hear *you* plainly. So Thank you Thora from (Mrs) Sallie Goodall
Dewsbury

Count your blessings, name them one by one,
Count your blessings, see what God has done,
Count your blessings, name them one by one,
And it will surprise you what the Lord has done!

Vera Littler from Bromley and Agnes Canniford from Exmouth each sent me slightly different variations of an extra verse for "Count your Blessings", so I'll give you both:

> Count your blessings, name them two by two,
> Count your blessings, name them four by four,
> Count your blessings, name them by the score,
> And it will surprise you there are hundreds more.

(and here's Vera's version)

> Count your blessings, name them two by two,
> Count your blessings, see what God can do,
> Count your blessings, name them by the score,
> And it will surprise you – there are *millions* more!

Christmas at Cheapside

Very often on **Praise Be!** we have the hymn "O for a Thousand Tongues to Sing". I love that hymn, but in my heart the tune, Lyngham, will always be associated with Christmas time. In Morecambe, when I was a child, the Salvation Army Band would march along Cheapside on Christmas morning every year, playing "Christians Awake" (and if any Christians weren't already awake – they soon were!) They'd always end with "While Shepherds Watched Their Flocks By Night", played to the tune of Lyngham. Some people say it doesn't fit, but it *does*, like this:

While Shepherds wa-a-a-a-atched their flo-ocks by-y
   night
All seated on the ground
All sea-ea-ea-ea-ea-ted on the ground
The angel o-o-of the Lo-o-ord came down
And glory shone (and glory shone) around
And glory sho-one (and glory sho-one) around
And glo-o-ory shone around

Ah yes! Happy days!

Cooking

Scotty is the Chef in our family, and his recipes have
helped to mend church spires, build extensions to church
rooms, help the aged, done their bit for Christian Aid and
even Saved the Children . . . Well, they have, you know!
Whenever anyone writes to ask me for a recipe for a book
they are making to raise money to repair their church roof
or for charity or for whatever it might be, I always send
them one of Scotty's best.

Here is my favourite, and he invented it when I was
working in the theatre and sometimes used to come home
too tired to want to eat. The smell of this dish cooking
was so marvellous, it woke up my appetite, and I could
always manage to eat it however late, however
exhausted.

Spaghetti Bake

2 large onions	3 oz long spaghetti
2 oz butter	2×4 oz cans peeled tomatoes
salt	6 oz strong cheddar cheese
pepper	sprigs of parsley
sage or mixed herbs	

1 Peel and slice the onions and fry in melted butter until tender and pale golden brown.
2 Arrange in ovenproof dish and season with salt, pepper and herbs.
3 Break dry spaghetti into 3" lengths, and scatter over top of onions.
4 Pour contents of cans of tomatoes over spaghetti, cutting them up if necessary.
5 Arrange grated cheese in even layer over top.
6 Cover with kitchen foil or lid and bake in a slow oven (Mark 2, 310 F.) for 1¼ hours. Remove foil or lid and return to moderately hot oven (375 or Mark 5) until golden brown (10 – 15 minutes)
7 Garnish with parsley and serve at once.

Christ

Christ is that bright morning star,
which, when the light of this world fails,
bringeth his saints to the joy of eternal life,
and to the light of everlasting day.

Venerable Bede (673–735)

I sometimes get letters from humanists and atheists (requesting their favourite hymns, too!), but the vast majority of people who write share, at the foundation of their lives, their faith in God and Jesus.

Christ is Made the Sure Foundation

Christ is made the sure foundation,
Christ the head and corner-stone,
Chosen of the Lord, and precious,
Binding all the Church in one,
Holy Zion's help for ever,
And her confidence alone.

To this temple, where we call Thee,
Come, O Lord of hosts, today:
With Thy wonted loving-kindness,
Hear Thy servants as they pray,
And Thy fullest benediction
Shed within its walls alway.

Here vouchsafe to all Thy servants
What they ask of Thee to gain,
What they gain from Thee for ever
With the blessed to retain,
And hereafter in Thy glory
Evermore with Thee to reign.

Laud and honour to the Father,
Laud and honour to the Son,
Laud and honour to the Spirit,
ever Three and ever One,

One in might, and One in glory,
While unending ages run.

Latin, Seventh century, translated by
John Mason Neale (1818–1886)

> And then my heart with pleasure fills
> And dances with the daffodils.

Wordsworth

Daffodils

Praise Be! is almost always shown in the spring or early summer, when Jan's garden is full of beautiful daffodils, which you may have noticed through the window behind me.

When the first little green shoots start breaking through the soil in January, I always say to Scotty, "the Praise Be letters will soon start arriving!"

Daisies

Another D flower is a daisy. Daisy, my granddaughter, is at university now, in America. James, her brother, is still at Lancing College in Sussex. They both seem to have grown up so quickly, I can hardly take it in.

Young people have so much more choice these days than we ever had, don't they? When Scotty and I were young, most of our generation just had to get on and make the best of things as they were. I don't mean we weren't happy. We were extremely happy, perhaps all the happier for *not* having too many choices to make. I wonder if perhaps we older people are sometimes not sympathetic enough about the difficulty for young people who have to make many important decisions so early on in life. What do you think?

Two years ago Daisy took part in a production of *Amahl and the Night Visitors*, which the Sussex Opera Company put on and toured round Sussex churches. Daisy played Amahl, a little lame shepherd boy, living in great poverty with his widowed mother, in a shack. One night three wise men, following a star from the east, on their way to Bethlehem, stop at Amahl's home. Amahl and his mother give up their meagre all to bring rest and refreshment to these visitors, and the story ends with Amahl no longer lame, on his way to see the new born baby Jesus for himself.

It's a real weepy, and of course, for Scotty, Jan and me, watching our own Daisy in the leading part, well, it was almost too much to bear. I don't know whether Daisy has made up her mind yet if she wants to become a professional actress – that's one of the choices she will have to make for herself. I do know that her annual birthday treat from me for the past few years – at her own request – has been a trip to the theatre. It seems only yesterday that I used to take little Jan, and now I take Jan's little girl, Daisy – and she's not so little!

Children and grandchildren who have left home and gone to live on the other side of the world are often the reason for viewers' requests for this next hymn. When you're getting up in the morning, you think of them saying their prayers and going to bed; and in the evenings, especially when there's a beautiful sunset, you remember that for them a new day is just beginning. I know that when Jan and the children were living in America, I always thought about them when we played this:

The Day Thou Gavest

The day Thou gavest, Lord, is ended,
The darkness falls at Thy behest;
To Thee our morning hymns ascended,
Thy praise shall sanctify our rest.

We thank Thee that thy Church unsleeping,
While earth rolls onward into light,
Through all the world her watch is keeping,
And rests not now by day or night.

As o'er each continent and island
The dawn leads on another day,
The voice of prayer is never silent,
nor dies the strain of praise away.

The sun that bids us rest is waking
Our brethren 'neath the western sky,
And hour by hour fresh lips are making
Thy wondrous doings heard on high.

So be it, Lord; Thy throne shall never,
Like earth's proud empires, pass away;
Thy kingdom stands, and grows for ever,
Till all Thy creatures own thy sway.

J. Ellerton (1826–1893)

Donkeys

Do you remember – if you saw it, I'm certain you will – **Songs of Praise** for Palm Sunday from Wells Cathedral a few years ago? It began inside the cathedral, which was completely empty – not just of people, but of chairs – everything – a huge space.

Then the great West doors were flung open and the organ struck up, and in walked a little donkey ridden by a child dressed as Jesus, and led by children singing ''Ride on, Ride on in majesty''. More and more children followed the donkey in, until the entire cathedral was full, and the singing, which had started with one or two voices, now swelled from thousands. I just thought I'd remind you. I've never forgotten it.

Praise Be! is usually made around Palm Sunday and Easter time, in the spring of the year, which is a donkey sort of time, I always think. When Jan was still living in Beverly Hills, and the children were small, I thought that there was no point in trying to get Easter Eggs out to them through the post, so I used to send money, that I would have spent on them, to the Donkey Sanctuary down in Devon, where they take in any donkey that has been neglected or cruelly treated. This year we shall visit the donkeys at the Sanctuary on **Praise Be!** (in April). I've always had a soft spot for donkeys, ever since I was a child and used to see them on the sands at Morecambe. I can still hear the sound of their little feet tapping over the cobbles when they came home in the evenings, and the men would let us help lead them along.

Do you know what would be the greatest treat for me? To be driven about in a little cart pulled by a donkey. Oh, I would love it!

I can't move on from D without reminding you that D is also for

Dogs (and Ducks)

Jan's dogs have had a big part to play in the making of **Praise Be!** over the years, and they get a lot of fan mail of their own! You can't walk round Jan's garden without a little procession forming, of ducks as well as dogs! Sadly, little Lucy, the Spaniel, died last year, so only Patch and Tess listened while I read one of the poems of the late Sister Maud of the Community of All Hallows, Ditchingham, Norfolk. Sister Maud wrote a marvellous little collection of thoughts, prayers and poems, *after* she had had her 80th birthday, kindly note!, which she called "Tailwags". This is Tailwag Number 1:

"Only the tail-end of life is left", I said;
And into my head
A thought came out of the blue;
A thought from You —
"But that is the cheery end", You said
"So see
That you use it for Me."
And I said "Amen" and raised my head,
"I WILL GLORIFY GOD WITH A WAG", I said!

Our animals and pets are sometimes silly, sometimes naughty, sometimes seriously bad, but we go on loving them. Does that give us a clue about how the Lord manages to go on loving us?!

Dear Lord and Father

Dear Lord and Father of mankind
Forgive our foolish ways
Reclothe us in our rightful mind
In purer lives thy service find
In deeper reverence praise.

In simple trust like theirs who heard,
Beside the Syrian sea,
The gracious calling of the Lord,
Let us, like them, without a word
Rise up and follow Thee.

O Sabbath rest by Galilee!
O calm of hills above,
Where Jesus knelt to share with Thee
The silence of Eternity
Interpreted by love!

Drop Thy still dews of quietness,
Till all our strivings cease;
Take from our souls the strain and stress,
And let our ordered lives confess
The beauty of Thy peace.

Breathe through the heats of our desire
Thy coolness and thy balm
Let sense be dumb, let flesh retire
Speak through the earthquake, wind and fire
O still small voice of calm.

                              J. G. Whittier (1807–1892)

Easter

I went to share with Him
His pain and loss
To understand His Cross
He met me in the glory of the skies
With laughter in His eyes.

Sister Maud CAH

Epitaphs

When I was making **In Loving Memory** with Yorkshire
Television, the writer, Dick Sharples, sometimes had to
invent funny epitaphs for my character, Ivy Unsworth,
who was an undertaker, to read out over the telephone
when she was helping people decide what to have
engraved on their loved ones' gravestones. This one got
a big laugh from the studio audience:

Goodbye, Granddad –
All the best.
The North lost a good'un
When you went west.

(Well, you have to hear me say it to get the best out of it!)

Sometimes reality is funnier than anything one could invent. We could easily have used this one on *In Loving Memory*, and not surprisingly, it comes from a Yorkshire churchyard:

> Underneath this stone doth lie,
> Back to back, my wife and I.
> When the last trump sounds so shrill,
> If she gets up, I'll lie still.

Then there's a story of a Yorkshireman who wanted an inscription on his wife's gravestone to read "She was Thine". The engraver mistakenly put "She was Thin". The man wrote saying they had missed the "E". The next effort read: "E, She was Thin"!

Of course, most epitaphs are serious and beautiful. You'll find one of the most moving, simple epitaphs on the memorial plaque for Robert Louis Stevenson in St Giles Cathedral, Edinburgh, lines from his own poem "Requiem":

> Under the wide and starry sky,
> Dig the grave and let me lie.
> Glad did I live and gladly die,
> And I laid me down with a will.
>
> This be the verse you grave for me:
> Here he lies where he longed to be;
> Home is the sailor, home from sea,
> And the hunter home from the hill.

Endings

Whenever possible, I like to end **Praise Be!** with a rousing, cheerful hymn, and some last happy thought or story to say goodbye on. I get a lot of ideas from parish magazines. Like the story of the little boy in Sunday School who had been asked to draw the Garden of Eden. He drew a nice garden with an apple tree, but he also drew a road in the garden, with a car and three people in it. The teacher said, "What's this car doing in Paradise, Peter?" And the little boy said, "That's Adam and Eve in the back, and that's God, in front, driving them out!"

Quite often the very last thing I say is "I'll be back next Sunday – D.V." This is because of a letter I received from a gentleman during one of the early series, which said, "You shouldn't say you'll be back next Sunday so confidently. It may not be the Lord's will that you should! You should say D.V." (Which means *Deo Volente* (or God Willing to you and me!) Well, he was right, you know!

Evening

Scotty and I love driving through the countryside together, sometimes stopping in a little village for a look round, and going into one of those olde worlde tea shops, with a copper kettle hanging outside, and home-made scones and cakes inside, and tea made with real leaves in a warmed up earthenware pot, none of your tea-bags, with a bit of string dangling out of the side! They're getting harder and harder to find these days, aren't they?

I can't drive myself, so when I'm in Yorkshire filming, if I get a couple of hours off, I like to hire a car and take anyone along with me who's also free, to go and explore. I especially enjoy visiting small country towns on market day, and looking round all the stalls. As a matter of fact, I'd like to make a television programme one of these days, about some of the funny things I've discovered on these little jaunts, like the red GPO telephone box that has been put right in the middle of a field of sheep! Fair's fair. It has to be there to be exactly equidistant between the three farmers who share it!

After a long summer's day you seem to come to a moment when time stops. Everything is warm, quiet and still, and the sun hovers motionless in the air before slipping away out of sight. I call it the time of day when God's putting his bedroom slippers on.

While he's doing it, just for those few seconds, you get a glimpse of Eternity.

Eternal Ruler of the Ceaseless Round

Eternal Ruler of the ceaseless round
Of circling planets singing on their way;
Guide of the nations from the night profound
Into the glory of the perfect day;
Rule in our hearts, that we may ever be
Guided and strengthened and upheld by Thee.

We are of Thee the children of Thy love,
The brothers of Thy well-beloved Son;

Descend, O Holy Spirit, like a dove
Into our hearts, that we may be as one:
As one with Thee, to whom we ever tend;
As one with Him, our brother and our friend.

We would be one in hatred of all wrong,
One in our love of all things sweet and fair,
One with the joy that breaketh into song,
One with the grief that trembleth into prayer,
One in the power that makes Thy children free
To follow truth, and thus to follow Thee.

O clothe us with Thy heavenly armour, Lord,
Thy trusty shield, Thy sword of love divine;
Our inspiration be Thy constant word;
We ask no victories that are not Thine:
Give or withhold, let pain or pleasure be;
Enough to know that we are serving Thee.

                    J. W. Chadwick (1840–1904)

Feeling the heat?
This place is Prayer Conditioned!

Families

When I was a child our family was Dad, James Henry
Hird, Mother, Mary Jane Mayor (Mayor until she married
Dad, that is), my sister Olga, who only had a very short
little life and died when she was six, brother Neville, and
last of the lot, me. Mother was the daughter of a
fisherman who trawled for shrimps in Morecambe Bay
along with my uncles, and Dad came from Todmorden
(the Lancashire side – half the town is in Yorkshire you
might know, and half in Lancashire); like Scotty, my Dad
also had forebears from Fife. My parents met in a touring
company.

I used to love hearing Mother's stories about those
days, on tour for several months at a time doing one night
stands, playing every county in the British Isles, the
young dandies who would crowd the stage door waiting
for the girls with bouquets of flowers. In fact, my mother
swore that my father would never have proposed had
it not been for the fact that one such young gentleman
waited for her at the stage door for four nights in
succession. I used to love the expression on her face as
she came out with the "curtain line" – "so, on the fifth

day, your father took me on a picnic and during our meal, he *proposed*!''

By the time I came along they had settled in Morecambe, at number 6 Cheapside, as I said, next door to the Royalty, where Dad was Stage Manager. People write and tell me how *their* family was the Happiest in the World, so I'll have to settle for saying that ours was One of the Happiest in the World.

My mother had a really beautiful mezzo-soprano voice and always sang the solo ''I know that my Redeemer Liveth'' when the *Messiah* was performed at the Green Street Wesleyan Chapel. Unfortunately I did not inherit her wonderful musical gift, and inspite of being made to practise the piano for an hour a day all through my childhood, I never really progressed beyond pieces written in two sharps. I like to feel that I made up for lack of skill with a certain brio and panache in my performance, but honesty forbids me from boasting of any real musical talent. I think my mother must be smiling in heaven to watch me presenting all the beautiful music we have on **Praise Be!** as though I were the great expert! Even Dad had joined Moore and Burgesses, an early version of the Black and White Minstrels, at the age of fifteen as a boy soprano.

Oh, but they were happy days. Dad on the banjo, Nev on the violin, Mother singing and Thora obliging on the pianoforte (in two sharps).

Today our family, still One of the Happiest in the World (of course), is composed of Scotty and me, our daughter, Jan, and her husband William, grandchildren Daisy and James, plus a great menagerie of Dogs, Ducks of every variety, Geese, Hens, and I believe that before too long we are to be joined by some Pigs, because – stand back! – ''Councillor'' Janette Scott Rademaekers (as we now have to address our daughter since she became a local councillor!) has been on a pig-keeping course recently.

Jan has always been soft about animals. I remember when she was a little girl we were living in another little cottage in the country, and there was a house martin's nest under the eaves. When the babies hatched out and started to learn to fly, she had me and Jimmy and her Nanny outside in the garden for hours, holding out the four corners of a big blanket as a safety net.

Many of our beautiful hymns remind us that Christians all belong to one big family, with God as our loving father.

Father, Hear the Prayer We Offer

Father, hear the prayer we offer;
Not for ease that prayer shall be,
But for strength that we may ever
Live our lives courageously.

Not for ever in green pastures
Do we ask our way to be;
But the steep and rugged pathway
May we tread rejoicingly.

Not for ever by still waters
Would we idly rest and stay;
But would smite the living fountains
From the rocks along our way.

Be our Strength in hours of weakness,
In our wanderings be our Guide;

Through endeavour, failure, danger,
Father, be thou at our side.

Mrs L. M. Willis (1864)

Friends

If you're lucky, and I have been, the friends you make
in your childhood and schooldays stay your friends all
through your life. I've always remained friends with all
my old class mates, and the people I knew who lived in
Cheapside in my youth. I can still recite the names of my
"best friends" from the Misses Nelson's school: Ada Lob,
Mabel Bagshaw, Una Yates, Kathy Mortimer, Lilian
Cross, Maudie Poles, Vera Muff, Madge Peel . . . Names
to conjure with! Even people I may not have seen for fifty
years still exchange Christmas cards with us. Sadly, the
number of old friends dwindles as the years go by, and
they move on to a better place than Cheapside, but Scotty
and I have been making friends all through our lives, and,
with our family, old and new friends together are our
greatest blessing.

Funerals

I do hope **Praise Be!** makes you feel happy. Naturally
some of the letters I receive come from people who are
feeling very sad, often because they are grieving over
someone who has just died. It's difficult, on a programme

watched by several million people, most of whom, thankfully, are not feeling at all sad, to speak to just one person who is in mourning. I do try to show that I have appreciated their letters and feel for them, and I hope that they understand.

No one who becomes at all familiar, through appearing on television, to thousands of people who they don't personally know, can expect to be understood or liked by everyone. Nor do any of us escape without receiving a few critical letters. I'm glad to say I haven't received many, because the ones I do receive have hurt me very much. So I think here might be a good place to talk a little bit about **In Loving Memory**. That's the comedy series where I played Ivy Unsworth, the owner of an old fashioned funeral parlour.

I don't myself make a division between my work as an actress, very often playing comedy roles, and my work as a presenter of **Praise Be!** I couldn't live a life in which I had to keep switching from being one kind of person to being another kind.

In Loving Memory was a very happy series. It was enjoyed by millions of people, none of whom thought for a moment that we were making fun of death or bereavement. Indeed, many of the appreciative letters we received came from people who had just lost someone, and the series had cheered and consoled them.

What we were making a little gentle fun of was the way most of us, let's face it, know very little about ritual. And yet we have to undergo this very formal ceremony when saying goodbye to our much beloved friends and relatives. So often when we are trying to be at our most solemn and dignified, however, something very comic happens, at which we would love to laugh, at which we *know* the person we are saying goodbye to would have laughed, but because of the solemnity we have imposed on ourselves, we feel we can't laugh. **In Loving Memory** released people from feeling guilty about having wanted to laugh, by showing them it is a normal human reaction.

So to the few, mercifully very few, people who wrote to tell me that I had no right whatever to present a Christian programme like **Praise Be!**, when I was acting in something so disrespectful as **In Loving Memory**, I can only say: I'm sorry, but I think you are mistaken.

I've chosen for **Praise Be!** over the years many prayers and poems to help people who are bereaved. None have touched people more than these beautiful words written by Canon Henry Scott Holland:

Death is nothing at all. I have only slipped away into the next room. I am I and you are you. Whatever we were to each other, that we are still.

Call me by my old familiar name, speak to me in the easy way which you always used. Put no difference into your tone; wear no forced air of solemnity or sorrow. Laugh as we always laughed at the little jokes we enjoyed together. Play, smile, think of me, pray for me.

Let my name be ever the household word that it always was, let it be spoken without an effort, without the trace of a shadow in it.

Life means all that it ever meant; it is the same as it ever was; there is absolutely unbroken continuity.

What is this death but a negligible accident? Why should I be out of mind because I am out of sight? I am just waiting for you, for an interval, somewhere very near, just around the corner. All is well.

Canon Henry Scott Holland (1847–1918)

You'd be surprised how many people write to request the hymn they've decided to have sung at their own funerals! This is one that is often selected.

Forth in Thy Name

Forth in Thy name, O Lord, I go,
My daily labour to pursue;
Thee, only Thee, resolved to know,
In all I think or speak or do.

The task Thy wisdom hath assigned
O let me cheerfully fulfil;
In all my works Thy presence find,
And prove Thy good and perfect will.

Thee may I set at my right hand,
Whose eyes my inmost substance see,
And labour on at Thy command,
And offer all my works to Thee.

Give me to bear Thy easy yoke,
And every moment watch and pray,
And still to things eternal look,
And hasten to Thy glorious day;

For Thee delightfully employ
Whate'er Thy bounteous grace hath given,
And run my course with even joy,
And closely walk with Thee to heaven.

Charles Wesley

Fishermen

Like my mother, I'm what we call in the North a Sand grown'un – someone born by the sea. We were both born in Morecambe. As I've said, my Grandfather and four uncles were fishermen who trawled for shrimps in Morecambe Bay. So hymns like "Eternal Father", "Will Your Anchor Hold", and "Pull for the shore, Sailor", always hold special memories for me.

I know I've mentioned on **Praise Be!** how, as a little girl, I once overheard someone saying to my Uncle Robert "Goodness, Robert, you look more like Jesus every day!" He had a black beard and always wore a navy blue fisherman's ganzie. After overhearing that, whenever I said my nightly prayers: "Gentle Jesus, meek and mild, look upon Thy little child, pity my simplicity, suffer me to come to Thee", I was saying it to Jesus wearing a fisherman's ganzie and cap.

One day, when I was a bit older, I said to my Mother: "Jesus doesn't really look like my Uncle Robert, does he?' She could see I was a little upset, and she just took my chin in her hands, kissed me on the forehead and said, "Who says he doesn't?"

If you're brought up by the sea as so many people are, living in a country which is also an island, you never lose your love of it. It brings you in touch with the power and beauty of nature, and when you stand by the sea, you feel you are looking out over the whole of our beautiful world.

For the Beauty of the Earth

For the beauty of the earth,
For the beauty of the skies,
For the love which from our birth
over and around us lies:
Lord of all, to Thee we raise
This our thankful hymn of praise

For the beauty of each hour
Of the day and of the night,
Hill and vale, and tree and flower,
Sun and moon and stars of light,
Lord of all, to Thee we raise
This our thankful hymn of praise

For the joy of ear and eye,
For the heart and mind's delight,
For the mystic harmony
Linking sense to sound and sight,
Lord of all, to Thee we raise
This our thankful hymn of praise

For the joy of human love,
Brother, sister, parent, child,
Friends on earth and friends above,
For all gentle thoughts and mild,
Lord of all, to Thee we raise
This our thankful hymn of praise

For each perfect gift of Thine
To our race so freely given,
Graces human and divine,

Flowers of earth and buds of heaven,
Lord of all, to Thee we raise
This our thankful hymn of praise

> F. S. Pierpoint (1835–1917)

God and Son
Soul Agents for this parish

Good News and Gospel Singing

Some years ago **Songs of Praise** came from Southwark Cathedral, in London, but instead of the usual congregation, it was filled with hundreds of choirs from different black gospel churches, dressed in their long robes, and the girls all wearing their lovely little hats. They looked like the cherubim and seraphim. You've never seen anything like it!

They made the cathedral vibrate, and they sang so – well, really they were joyous. They used their whole bodies, and their hearts and voices, swaying and clapping and jumping up and down. They reminded me that hymn-singing is not a sad, onerous duty, which, I'm sorry to say, sometimes seems to be the case in parish churches on a Sunday morning, and occasionally even on **Songs of Praise**. Hymns are about good news, very good news, and singing them is a celebration . . .

Great is Thy Faithfulness

Great is Thy faithfulness, O God my Father,
There is no shadow of turning with Thee;
Thou changest not, Thy compassions they fail not,
As Thou hast been Thou for ever wilt be.

Great is Thy faithfulness!
Great is Thy faithfulness!
Morning by morning new mercies I see;
All I have needed Thy hand hath provided, –
Great is Thy faithfulness, Lord, unto me!

Summer and winter, and springtime and harvest,
Sun, moon and stars in their courses above,
Join with all nature in manifold witness
To Thy great faithfulness, mercy and love.

Pardon for sin and a peace that endureth,
Thine own dear presence to cheer and to guide;
Strength for today and bright hope for tomorrow,
Blessings all mine, with ten thousand beside!

T. O. Chisholm (1866–1960)

The Good Old Days

When were these good old days, do you suppose? And
were they always quite as good as people think they
remember? When some people talk about the good old
days, they are talking about an age before even I was
born. Or your good old days may be my quite recent past.

Some people might say that "in the Good Old Days Thora used to present **Praise Be!** from a studio, wearing a long evening dress and a rose in her bosom." (It's true! That's how we did it for the first two years. I used to sit on a hard-back chair, a tiny dot in the middle of a huge studio, at the Television Centre, with three or four cameras shooting me from every angle, wearing a long satin evening dress with a rose in the cleavage. Nowadays I sit in the comfort of my daughter's home, with a single camera, and wearing my every-day clothes.)

Anyway, I hope I haven't given the impression that I live in the past, and think everything's gone down hill since the Good Old Days. Nothing could be further from the truth. All my life I've been happy, and in nearly every way things have gone on getting better and better.

But − I was happy when I was a child, and many of the dearest people in the world, my mother, my father, my brother Nev, who belonged to my own good old days, have gone. Even today, in the Good New Days, when something wonderful happens, like the tremendous honour of receiving the OBE a few years ago, or more recently, when I won the BAFTA award for Alan Bennett's play *Cream Cracker Under the Sofa*, I find myself wishing so much that they could all still be here, just so I could say to them: "It's because of you that things have turned out so well for me, all the teaching you gave me, all the love."

My mother, in particular, gave us so much love, and it's a fairly common experience, I suppose, to find that when you come to a stage in your life when you could really give something back, and make life easier for her, it's too late.

God be with you till we meet again

God be with you till we meet again,
By His counsels guide, uphold you,
With His sheep securely fold you:
God be with you till we meet again.

God be with you till we meet again,
'Neath His wings protecting hide you,
Daily manna still provide you:
God be with you till we meet again.

God be with you till we meet again,
When life's perils thick confound you,
Put His arms unfailing round you:
God be with you till we meet again.

God be with you till we meet again,
Keep love's banner floating o'er you,
Smile death's threatening wave before you:
God be with you till we meet again.

Jeremiah Eames Rankin (1824–1904)

Holy

Holy, Holy, Holy, Lord God of Hosts
Heaven and earth are full of Your glory!

Harvest Festival

I know I've told this story before on **Praise Be!**, for it
always comes back to me when we're getting ready for
Harvest Thanksgiving.

Scott and Jan and I were in the little village of Preston
Bissett, in Buckinghamshire, in a pub called the Old Hat.
The local vicar was holding his Harvest Festival service
right there, in the pub. All the old country fellows were
supping their ale, and they all knew him. The bar had
been done up with flowers, fruit and vegetables, huge
marrows and such like.

I remember he came from the Lake District, this vicar,
and was a countryman himself. He told us how these
days scientists were discovering, inventing and making
more and more wonderful things, bigger and better
machines, cleverer computers, and generally coming up
with things nobody would have even dreamed of a few
years ago.

Then I remember he said, ''But you show me the
scientist who knows how to make a seed. An ordinary,

tiny little seed, like you all sowed a million of last spring, which is why we've got this beautiful harvest. And if you can find the man who can make you a seed – which you can't – but if you can, you plant it, and then come and tell me what comes up!''

Hedgehogs

Another visit I made to Buckinghamshire, this time for **Praise Be!**, I wouldn't have missed for the world. It was to Sue and Les Stocker's Wildlife Hospital, which they ran from their own home on a housing estate in Aylesbury. It was a very respectable neighbourhood, but just outside their backdoor lived two badgers, two herons, a hare, a rabbit, some bats, a blind stoat, some owls, tortoises, dormice, deer, ducks . . . over two hundred animals on any one day, and one whole section, called St Tiggiwinkles, devoted entirely to injured hedgehogs.

It was a magical place. The diningroom was the office, the garden shed housed medical equipment, drips and incubators, another outhouse formed the Intensive Care Unit.

Since then more and more people have come to know about the wonderful work Sue and Les do in rescuing and caring for wild animals which have been injured, nearly always because of us humans, and now they have been able to expand, buy some land, and put up purpose-designed buildings, where they are establishing a Wildlife Teaching Hospital.

Hedgehogs are such funny, primitive looking creatures,

aren't they? I held one little one, injured by a car, as so many of them are, and he looked at me with his beady eyes, and I thought he was saying, "We hedgehogs have been around much longer than you johnny-come-lately humans. We're not changing our old ways and haunts just for you." But I expect he just wanted me to let him go back to sleep!

How Great Thou Art

O Lord my God! When I in awesome wonder
Consider all the works Thy hand hath made,
I see the stars, I hear the mighty thunder,
Thy power throughout the universe displayed:

Then sings my soul, my Saviour God, to Thee,
How great Thou art! How great Thou art!
Then sings my soul, my Saviour God, to Thee,
How great Thou art! How great Thou art!

When through the woods and forest glades I wander
And hear the birds sing sweetly in the trees;
When I look down from lofty mountain grandeur,
And hear the brook, and feel the gentle breeze:

And when I think that God, His Son not sparing,
Sent Him to die – I scarce can take it in.
That on the cross, my burden gladly bearing,
He bled and died to take away my sin:

When Christ shall come with shouts of acclamation
And take me home – what joy shall fill my heart!

Then shall I bow in humble adoration
And there proclaim, my God, how great Thou art!

Then sings my soul, my Saviour God, to Thee,
How great Thou art! How great Thou art!
Then sings my soul, my Saviour God, to Thee,
How great Thou art! How great Thou art!

Translated from the Russian by
Stuart K. Hine c. 1953

Holmfirth

Some other "rural" characters who have come into my
life in recent years are the wonderful cast of **Last of the
Summer Wine**. They have all been very welcoming and
kind to me, the new girl. Before I ever knew I was going
to join them, I visited Holmfirth for **Praise Be!**, and sat
in the cafe there, talking to Joe Gladwyn, who played
Norah Batty's husband Wally.

He was a wonderful Christian man, Joe, who did so
much work for charity in his spare time, and had been
awarded a Papal Medal, of which he was very proud. I'm
very glad he came on **Praise Be!** and talked so simply
about his faith, because he died a year later, and we do
miss him so. He was a happy man, who loved God.

Happy are They

Happy are they, they that love God,
Whose hearts have Christ confest,
Who by His Cross have found their life,
And 'neath His yoke their rest.

Glad is the praise, sweet are the songs,
When they together sing;
And strong the prayers that bow the ear
Of heaven's eternal King.

Christ to their homes giveth His peace,
And makes their loves His own:
But ah, what tares the evil one
Hath in His garden sown!

Sad were our lot, evil this earth,
Did not its sorrows prove
The path whereby the sheep may find
The fold of Jesus' love.

Then shall they know, they that love Him,
How all their pain is good;
And death itself cannot unbind
Their happy brotherhood.

Yattendon Hymnal

> I grumbled when I had no shoes
> Until I met a man who had no feet.

(We keep this little notice at the head of our stairs at home, so I can't fail to read it every day. It's a great mindjerker.)

Icons

> I ask not to see
> I ask not to know
> I ask simply to be used
>
> Cardinal Newman

I was brought up in the Methodist chapel. These days I don't mind which church or chapel I go to, and more often than not it's the little Church of England parish church near our home. But I was definitely brought up in what you might call the Protestant Tradition.

These days, although services in different denominations still have very varied styles and character, depending on whether they are Evangelical, Charismatic, Pentecostal, Baptist, Quaker, U.R.C., Methodist, High, Low or Middle of the Road Anglican, Roman Catholic, Russian or Greek Orthodox, there has been a sort of Perestroika, or Glasnost, between the different churches, and a lot more is shared and enjoyed together. A Roman

Catholic mass is no longer incomprehensible to us Protestant visitors, and many Roman Catholics seem to enjoy joining in with our hymn- and Bible-based services.

Russian and Greek Orthodox services are harder to follow without quite a detailed initiation, particularly if you don't speak Russian or Greek. Their icons are prayerfully painted images of religious figures, especially of Mary and Jesus, full of symbolism, and may seem rather strange to Protestant eyes, but more people are beginning to turn to them in their spiritual life, and no longer think of them as a blasphemous transgression of the Commandment ''Thou shalt not make any graven image''.

I can't see myself ever standing and praying in front of an icon, but if they help someone to understand that the face of God is a loving face, well, as my mother would have said, they're not hurting anybody are they? And God sent us Jesus, the most beautiful icon of all.

Hymns are sort of word icons, you might say. They try to express things which you can hardly put into words.

Immortal, Invisible

Immortal, invisible, God only wise,
In light inaccessible hid from our eyes,
Most blessed, most glorious, the Ancient of Days,
Almighty, victorious, Thy great name we praise.

Unresting, unhasting, and silent as light,
Nor wanting, nor wasting, thou rulest in might;

Thy justice like mountains high soaring above
Thy clouds which are fountains of goodness and love.

To all life Thou givest – to both great and small;
In all life Thou livest, the true life of all;
We blossom and flourish as leaves on the tree,
And wither and perish – but nought changeth Thee.

Great Father of Glory, pure Father of Light,
Thine Angels adore Thee, all veiling their sight;
All laud we would render: O help us to see
'Tis only the splendour of light hideth Thee.

W. Chalmers Smith (1824–1908)

Interviews

Mostly on **Praise Be!** I introduce the hymns from in front
of a television set at home, so I can enjoy them too. Now
and again I go out and about to visit the places where
famous hymns were written or inspired, like the cleft rock
of Burrington Combe in the Mendips, where the
Reverend Augustus Toplady was said to have sheltered,
and found the inspiration for that very famous hymn
"Rock of Ages".

   In 1989 I went to Horbury Bridge, where Sabine Baring-
Gould wrote my favourite, "Onward Christian Soldiers",
for his Sunday School children to sing in a Whitsunday
procession. I said on the film that I wondered what those
children had made of "Onward Christian Soldiers",
singing it for the very first time. I was delighted to receive
this letter the next day from Kathleen Tomlinson, from
Hornsea, North Humberside:

I can tell you what one small 5 year old boy thought, as he was my Grandfather, Albert Edward Rhodes. It thrilled him so much that he never forgot for the rest of his life, and he lived to be 92!

. . . He was a real Christian Soldier and a Christian gentleman, much loved by his children, grandchildren and great- grandchildren, and held in great esteem in the Community. I'm sure that the walk, the hymn and Rev. Sabine Baring- Gould had a great effect on his life.

At other times I visit someone who also loves hymns and we have a little chat, usually over a cup of coffee. It's not really an interview, as such, because nine times out of ten the person is a good friend of mine already, although I have met and made some wonderful new friends as well.

One of the people I called in on last year was Cheerful Charlie Chester. What a nice chap! We were talking about the war, and he suddenly came out with this poem that he'd made up in his head one night when he was on sentry duty.

The Sentry

So you've come to the end of your journey, soldier,
And you say you've been brave and true.
Well they're not the qualities I need, my friend,
Before I can pass you through.
You say that you've merits outstanding in battle,
And righteous wars must be won.
But have you had courage to pray to our Lord,
For the sins that you neednot have done?

You pause at my challenge, dear soldier.
Of weapons I've none in my hand,
For I am the sentry Saint Peter,
And this is my Maker's own land.
And to pass to the life everlasting
You must prove beyond word of a doubt,
Whether or no, you're our friend or our foe,
To find sanctuary here – or cast out.

You are still standing upright, dear soldier,
You seem not afraid at my quest.
There is no need to answer me, soldier.
I can see that your soul is at rest.
And for courage and loyalty, soldier,
In resisting the talons of hell
We offer – not medals – but peace everlasting,
So, soldier – PASS FRIEND – ALL'S WELL.

Charlie Chester
(as recited by him on **Praise Be!** 1989)

"In heavenly love abiding" is a hymn about confidence.

Have I told you the story about the man out walking
with his dog in the town, who met some friends? While
he was chatting to them, his dog wandered off on his
own. The man finished his conversation, realized the dog
had left him, so went off to look for him. He found him
cowering at the end of a long, dark alley way, with a lot
of rough louts throwing stones at him. The man stood
at the entrance and called out, "Shep! Here boy!" When
the dog heard his master's voice, even though he couldn't
see him, and was still on his own, he got his courage back
and went "WOOF! WOOF!" very loudly at the boys,

who ran off, afraid. This hymn gives us all that kind of confidence, knowing that God is near – but don't all start barking at once!

In Heavenly Love Abiding

In heavenly love abiding
No change my heart shall fear,
And safe is such confiding,
For nothing changes here:
The storm may roar without me,
My heart may low be laid;
But God is round about me,
And can I be dismayed?

Wherever He may guide me,
No want shall turn me back;
My Shepherd is beside me,
And nothing can I lack:
His wisdom ever waketh,
His sight is never dim;
He knows the way He taketh,
And I will walk with Him.

Green pastures are before me,
Which yet I have not seen:
Bright skies will soon be o'er me,
Where the dark clouds have been.
My hope I cannot measure,
My path to life is free;
My Saviour has my treasure,
And He will walk with me.

Anna Laetitia Waring (1820–1910)

Joy

You shall go out with joy
and be led forth with peace,
and the mountains and the hills
shall break forth before you.
There will be shouts of joy –
and the trees of the field shall clap their hands
and you'll go out with joy.

S. Dauermann (in *Mission Praise*)
© 1975 Lillenas Publishing Co.

Journeys

Religion should be the road you walk along, not the fortress you hide inside, least of all your prison. One of the best things, I think, about Pasolini's film, *The Gospel According to Matthew*, is the way it shows Jesus always on the move, walking very fast from place to place. And if you work it out, Jesus must have travelled immense distances, up and down the country from region to region, town to town, village to village, and finally, his last journey, up to the great city of Jerusalem. His followers were sometimes a little straggle of men trying to keep up, sometimes a huge crowd.

Stories about people on journeys and the rules of the

road must have often come into Jesus' mind while He was dong so much travelling Himself.

You probably think of this next story as being the one about The Good Samaritan, but an important part of the story is that it is about people on journeys.

The Journey from Jerusalem Down to Jericho

Jesus said:

"A man was going down from Jerusalem to Jericho, when he fell into the hands of robbers. They stripped him of his clothes, beat him and went away, leaving him half-dead.

"A priest happened to be going down the same road, and when he saw the man, he passed by on the other side.

"So too, a Levite, when he came to the place and saw him, passed by on the other side.

"But a Samaritan, as he travelled, came where the man was; and when he saw him, he took pity on him. He went to him and bandaged his wounds, pouring on oil and wine. Then he put the man on his own donkey, brought him to an inn and took care of him. The next day he took out two silver coins and gave them to the inn-keeper. 'Look after him,' he said, 'and when I return, I will reimburse you for any extra expense you may have.'

"Which of these three do you think was a neighbour to the man who fell into the hands of robbers?"

The expert in the law replied, "The one who had mercy on him." Jesus told him, "Go and do likewise."

Luke 10: 30–37 (NIV)

Certain hymns seem to touch a chord in all of us – not *just* the members of Women's Institutes!

Jerusalem

And did those feet in ancient time
Walk upon England's mountains green?
And was the holy Lamb of God
On England's pleasant pastures seen?
And did the countenance divine
Shine forth upon our clouded hills?
And was Jerusalem builded here
Among those dark satanic mills?

Bring me my bow of burning gold!
Bring me my arrows of desire!
Bring me my spear! O clouds unfold!
Bring me my chariot of fire!
I will not cease from mental fight,
Nor shall my sword sleep in my hand,
Till we have built Jerusalem
In England's green and pleasant land.

William Blake (1757–1827)

Jokes

No jokes please, we're Christians.

I've never seen a painting of Jesus laughing. Have you? And yet Jesus is the image of God, the creator, and creation is full of laughter, full of jokes.

Nearly all animals and birds are the same as us. Much of their life is a serious matter of hard work and making sure they survive. But in their family groups, they play tricks, and tease one another, and play – which even if you don't live in the country, you'll have seen on television wild-life programmes. Joking is part of love.

A group of mentally handicapped men who live in Margate were taken along by the lady who looks after them to the local vicar, because she wanted them to join his confirmation classes. (This is a true story I'm telling you.) He was very pleased to have them, but he found that whenever he read to them from the gospels, they would collapse with laughter. It all started when he told them Jesus' story about a king who gave a great banquet, and one by one the invited guests made excuses not to come, one saying he had just bought a field and wanted to go and look at it, another saying he'd got five new oxen and was just on his way to try them out, and finally the one who said he'd just got married, so of course, he wouldn't be coming . . . . Well, these men rolled about the floor weeping with laughter, and ever after that he only had to mention the name Jesus to set them off again. They thought Jesus was even funnier than Rabbi Lionel Blue!

Do you think they may have seen something we've missed!

Whoever we are, even if we have missed the point of some of his best jokes, God wants us to come to Him.

Just as I Am

Just as I am, without one plea
But that Thy blood was shed for me
And that Thou bidst me come to Thee
O Lamb of God, I come.

Just as I am, though tossed about
With many a conflict, many a doubt,
Fightings within and fears without,
O Lamb of God, I come.

Just as I am, poor, wretched, blind;
Sight, riches, healing of the mind,
Yea all I need, in Thee to find,
O Lamb of God, I come.

Just as I am, Thou wilt receive,
Wilt welcome, pardon, cleanse, relieve:
Because Thy promise I believe,
O Lamb of God, I come.

Just as I am (Thy love unknown
Has broken every barrier down),
Now to be Thine, yea, Thine alone,
O Lamb of God, I come.

Just as I am, of that free love
The breadth, length, depth, and height to prove,
Here for a season, then above,
O Lamb of God, I come.

Charlotte Elliott (1789–1871)

The kingdom of heaven is like to a grain
of mustard seed.

Keepsakes and Kindnesses

Sometimes a keepsake isn't the most precious or
expensive thing you own. I'm back thinking about my
mother again. It's funny how often I do.

I remember going on a picnic with the school nature-
study class, when I was about eight years old. I had been
given sixpence to spend, and after the picnic of banana
sandwiches, wedge of cake and an apple, I visited the
tiny village shop at Wennington to have a look round and
choose presents to take back to the family – which we
always did. Dad's present was five Woodbines (2d), and
Neville got a real slate pencil (1d). After a lot of deep
thought, my present for my mother was a little necklace
stamped out of celluloid with a pendant hanging from
it. I spent a very long time choosing that pendant, because
there were quite a few designs, each with different hand-
painted pictures on them. At long last I plumped for a
small oval one that had a little cupid, with rather a
quizzical expression on his face, painted on it. With the
remaining penny I think I bought myself some aniseed
balls.

The reason I'm telling you all this – and I agree it does

seem to be taking me rather a time to get to the point —
is that on the Friday after my gifts had been given and
received with great pleasure, my parents were invited out
to dinner by some friends. When my mother was all
dressed and ready to go, she came upstairs to kiss us
good night and God bless, a thing she never failed to do.
When she leaned over to kiss me as I lay in bed,
something lightly tickled my chin — it was the pendant!
She was wearing it! My pendant! Bought with my
threepence! What a brave woman, a lovely brown crepe-
de-chine dress, tiny pearl earrings, and a threepenny
pendant! No wonder Cupid was looking slightly
quizzical!

The Kingdom of God

Soon afterwards He went on through cities and villages
preaching and bringing good news of the Kingdom of
God.
And the twelve were with Him, and also some
women . . .

Luke 8: 1–2

. . . and when I think about the Kingdom of God, which
Jesus said was like the tiniest grain of mustard seed,
which would grow into a tree so big, the birds would nest
in its branches, I think of home, and my mother.

The King of Love

The King of love my shepherd is,
His goodness faileth never;
I nothing lack while I am His
And he is mine forever.

Where streams of living water flow
My ransomed soul He leadeth,
And where the verdant pastures grow
With food celestial feedeth.

Perverse and foolish oft I strayed,
But yet in love He sought me,
And on his shoulder gently laid,
And home, rejoicing, brought me.

In death's dark vale I fear no ill
With Thee, dear Lord, beside me;
Thy rod and staff my comfort still,
Thy Cross before to guide me.

Thou spread'st a table in my sight;
Thy unction grace bestoweth:
And O what transport of delight
From thy pure chalice floweth!

And so through all the length of days
Thy goodness faileth never;
Good Shepherd, may I sing Thy praise
Within Thy house for ever!

> The 23rd Psalm, adapted by
> Sir H. W. Baker
> (1821–1877)

Laughter

Whatever else you do or forbear,
impose upon yourself the task of happiness;
and now and then abandon yourself
to the joy of laughter.

Max Ehrmann
(© 1976 Robert L. Bell
Melrose, Mass., USA)

Laughter is the best antidote for tears.

Lucille Ball

Letters

As I said at the beginning, the letters viewers send to
Praise Be! are what make it such a pleasure to work on,
and to watch (yes, well, Scotty and I watch it too,
remember!).

In the earliest programmes I didn't play requests. We
chose certain themes, and included hymns from **Songs
of Praise** which fitted those themes. But very soon I was
receiving so many letters during and after the series, from
people telling me all about *their* favourite hymns, that we
thought it would be better to leave it to them in future!
Now, when I pop briefly onto the air after **Songs of Praise**

in January and February to remind viewers that it's time to start writing in with their requests, I never get less than four thousand letters in reply, and sometimes as many as ten thousand arrive.

I love receiving them, but they take a very long time to read, and I can only answer a few of them. I know this disappoints some people, but I think they understand that my best way of replying to them is to include the hymns they've asked for on **Praise Be!**

Dear Thora,
Thank you so much for your lovely, lovely services. They mean so much to me as I haven't been able to go to church for over three years and miss them so much. The singing is lovely, and I so like hearing the letters read out.

When you are bedridden you are so blessed with time to pray for other people, and you'd be surprised how many friends I have made through prayer!

I fear there is no prospect of my ever getting better. Never mind. The spirit is strong and I have a lovely husband, and wonderful friend who look after me wonderfully. I have a lovely son who is a vicar in East Anglia, so I am very blessed.
God bless you, dear Thora
Love, Barbara Newtons
Etchingham

Dear Thora,
Thank you for the hymn "The Lord's My Shepherd" included on **Praise Be!** yesterday.

Just came at the right time for us. I have my six-monthly check up at Radio Therapy Dept. this

week. I want to celebrate our Ruby Wedding next
June. I do have a lot of Faith, but sometimes you
find yourself afraid.
Many thanks, for all you do in the programme.
Yours sincerely,
Audrey Snow
Leicester

I'm sure Audrey, and the many hundreds like her who
have requested this hymn, know all the words by heart.

The Lord's My Shepherd

The Lord's my Shepherd, I'll not want
He makes me down to lie
In pastures green; He leadeth me
The quiet waters by.

My soul He doth restore again;
And me to walk doth make
Within the paths of righteousness,
Ev'n for His own name's sake.

Yea, though I walk in death's dark vale,
Yet will I fear none ill:
For Thou art with me; and Thy rod
And staff me comfort still.

My table Thou hast furnished
In presence of my foes;
My head Thou dost with oil anoint,
And my cup overflows.

Goodness and mercy all my life
Shall surely follow me:
And in God's house for evermore
My dwelling-place shall be.

The 23rd Psalm – metric version

Love

There are so many beautiful readings in the Bible about love, aren't there? None more so than this passage in St Paul's first letter to the Corinthians. I don't think that any modern translation can match the Authorized Version, which so many of us were brought up on. I'm not one to be against modern translations, in fact, I usually prefer them, but there are some parts of the Bible that were written first in such a beautiful way that they just seem to haunt your memory forever.

"Charity" means love, even though nowadays we only use it in a narrower sense, to mean giving money to good causes. If we do that without love there doesn't seem much point to it, does there!

Jan read 1 Corinthians 13 on **Praise Be!** a couple of years ago, when love was our theme.

Though I speak with the tongues of men and of angels, and have not charity, I am become as sounding brass, or a tinkling cymbal.

And though I have the gift of prophecy, and understand all mysteries, and all knowledge; and though I have all faith, so that I could remove mountains, and have not charity, I am nothing.

And though I bestow all my goods to feed the poor, and though I give my body to be burned, and have not charity, it profiteth me nothing.

Charity suffereth long, and is kind; charity envieth not, charity vaunteth not itself, is not puffed up.

Doth not behave itself unseemly, seeketh not her own, is not easily provoked, thinketh no evil;

Rejoiceth not in iniquity, but rejoiceth in the truth;

Beareth all things, believeth all things, hopeth all things, endureth all things,

Charity never faileth: but whether there be prophecies, they shall fail; whether there be tongues, they shall cease; whether there be knowledge, it shall vanish away.

For we know in part, and we prophesy in part.

But when that which is perfect is come, then that which is in part shall be done away.

When I was a child, I spake as a child, I understood as a child, I thought as a child: but when I became a man, I put away childish things.

For now we see through a glass, darkly; but then face to face: now I know in part; but then shall I know as also I am known.

And now abideth faith, hope, charity, these three; but the greatest of these is charity.

First Letter to the Corinthians 13 (AV)

So many of the letters I receive on **Praise Be!** are requests for hymns people sang at their weddings. You know, all the usual, appropriate ones: ''Through the night of doubt and sorrow'', ''Fight the Good Fight . . .''

No, I'm only kidding. No hymn is more often asked for, to bring back memories of a happy wedding day, than Charles Wesley's beautiful: "Love Divine".

Love Divine

Love Divine, all loves excelling
Joy of heaven, to earth come down.
Fix in us Thy humble dwelling
All Thy faithful mercies crown.
Jesu, Thou art all compassion,
Pure unbounded love Thou art;
Visit us with Thy salvation,
Enter every trembling heart.

Come, Almighty, to deliver,
Let us all Thy life receive;
Suddenly return, and never,
Never more Thy temples leave.
Thee we would be always blessing,
Serve Thee as Thy hosts above,
Pray, and praise Thee, without ceasing,
Glory in Thy perfect love.

Finish then Thy new creation,
Pure and spotless let us be;
Let us see Thy great salvation,
Perfectly restored in Thee,
Changed from glory into glory,
Till in heaven we take our place,
Till we cast our crowns before Thee,
Lost in wonder, love, and praise!

C. Wesley (1707–1788)

May you be in heaven half an hour
before the Divil knows you're dead!

Irish blessing

Master Carpenter
– Needs Joiners!

Morecambe

My mother, Mary Jane Mayor, was a Methodist born in
Morecambe; I myself was born and married in
Morecambe on mornings in May. So you can see that M
is a major letter for me!

You might be wondering, since I do go on about how
much I love Morecambe, why I should have lived for the
past fifty years in London, and even our country cottage
is in Sussex. Well, one reason is that Morecambe, the real
Morecambe that is, the one you can all visit any
Wednesday, and they won't even charge you for it, is
a wonderful place, but it's not exactly *my* Morecambe any
longer. "My" Morecambe exists only in my memories.

You have only to think of our old way of enjoying
Morecambe Carnival, the illuminations sparkling from
lamp post to lamp post, while the flower beds in the
promenade gardens were a mass of twinkling lights. (This
magical effect was achieved by placing thousands of night
lights in little coloured glass jars. They were replaced and

lit each evening by hordes of volunteers armed with tapers and matches.) Well, I'm here to tell you, they don't do it like that in Morecambe these days!

In my day, as the rows of revellers walked arm in arm along the promenade they would sing the Carnival Anthem:

Dear old Morecambe – more come to Morecambe by the sea,
There's good fresh air – from Heysham up to Bare,
Jollity everywhere. So, throw away your care
And come to dear old Morecambe
Here's to its prosperity
Folks don't die and that's the reason why
More come to Morecambe by the sea!

Sophisticated? Don't talk to me about sophistication!

Of course, I do go back there, to today's Morecambe, I mean. I had a lovely visit when I went to take part in **Songs of Praise**, and for **Praise Be!**, and for **Favourite Things** (another television programme, you might know), and Scotty and I go back to see old friends. Our very first home, "Prompt Corner", which we bought brand new for the amazing sum of four hundred and ninety-five pounds, is still there – though I think if you offered to buy it today they might want a bit more for it! But there's no Cheapside, no Royalty Theatre, and as for the Central Pier Pavilion, well that burnt down on 31st July 1933, and I still get a lump in my throat thinking about it.

The Morecambe I go on about is the Morecambe inside my heart, and that Morecambe I'll never leave.

I expect you all have a "Morecambe", where you were born and grew up and enjoyed all the bright golden mornings of childhood.

Morning has Broken

Morning has broken like the first morning;
Blackbird had spoken like the first bird:
Praise for the morning, praise for the singing
Praise for them springing fresh from the word!

Sweet the rain's new fall, sunlit from heaven,
Like the first dew fall on the first grass:
Praise for the sweetness of the wet garden,
Sprung in completeness where His feet pass.

Mine is the sunlight, mine is the morning
Born of the one light Eden saw play:
Praise with elation, praise every morning,
God's recreation of the new day!

Eleanor Farjeon (1881–1965)
(© David Higham Associates Ltd)

Mary

So many of the letters I receive contain phrases like ''My mother, God bless her . . .'' or ''My best friend, my mother. . .'', and as you will have realized by now, my own mother meant the world to me, so I can quite understand anyone who, even in their sixties and seventies, still talks about missing their mother.

Jesus' mother, Mary, holds a special place in our hearts because we can all understand and sympathize with her. How dreadful it must have been for her on that day when they were all out together as a family, going on a pilgrimage to the Holy City of Jerusalem, when Jesus was still just a little lad, and Mary suddenly realized that he was no longer with them, and that she must have lost Him in the crowd. I think nearly every mother at some time goes through the experience of thinking they've somehow lost or endangered their own child.

Just like our own loving Mums, Jesus' mother was His most loyal and faithful supporter all along. And when you think, He was the Son of God, but even at the end, dying on the cross, at the very climax of all He had come to do, He was still concerned for her.

No, I don't think any of us need feel ashamed about missing our mothers.

And in family life, when there's a quarrel, isn't it so often our mothers who are the peacemakers? St Francis of Assisi sometimes used to say that he felt like "a mother" to his brothers.

Make Me a Channel

Make me a channel of your peace.
Where there is hatred let me bring Your love
Where there is injury, your pardon, Lord;
And where there's doubt, true faith in You.
Oh, Master, grant that I may never seek
so much to be consoled, as to console;
to be understood, as to understand;
to be loved, as to love with all my soul.

Make me a channel of your peace.
Where there's despair in life, let me bring hope;
Where there is darkness, only light;
And where there's sadness, ever joy.
Oh, Master, grant that I may never seek
so much to be consoled, as to console.
to be understood, as to understand;
to be loved, as to love with all my soul.

Make me a channel of your peace.
It is in pardoning that we are pardoned,
In giving to all men that we receive;
And in dying that we're born to eternal life.

Prayer of St Francis
© 1967 Franciscan Communications

Neighbours

"Love the Lord your God with all your heart, with all
your soul, and with all your mind." This is the greatest
and the most important commandment.

The second most important commandment is like it:
"Love your neighbour as you love yourself."

Matthew 22: 37–39 (Good News Bible)

Neighbours

No, no, I don't mean "Nei-ei-eighbours"! I mean our
own British, next-door kind. In the North people are often
known, not by their names, but by their position in your
street. "Next-door want to know if they can borrow the
wheel-barrow. Haven't Opposite got it? Or did we lend
it to Three Down last?" Yes, honestly!

I can't imagine a life without being on friendly and
"helping out" terms with the people living round about,
because that's the way I was brought up and we've lived
like that ever since. Even in central London, we have
smashing neighbours in our Mews; and down in Sussex,
even though we can't be there as often as we'd like,
through our daughter, Jan, who loves it so much she's
even become a local Councillor, we know nearly everyone
in the village.

Neighbours aren't friends you've carefully selected for the things you have in common, or for their wit or attractiveness, or the high moral tone they lend to the neighbourhood. The neighbours are just the funny mixed bag of people with whom you happen to share a street, a block of flats, a mews or a village. You get to know one another, and become friends, because you know, for better or worse, you're all in the same boat, and life will be better for everyone if you all pull together. And if that means you having to put up with their funny ways, remember, they're also putting up with yours!

When I Needed a Neighbour

When I needed a neighbour, were you there, were you
    there?
When I needed a neighbour, were you there?
And the creed and the colour and the name won't
    matter,
Were you there?

I was hungry and thirsty, were you there, were you
    there?
I was hungry and thirsty, were you there?
And the creed and the colour and the name won't
    matter,
Were you there?

I was cold, I was naked, were you there, were you
    there?
I was cold, I was naked, were you there?

And the creed and the colour and the name won't
matter,
Were you there?

When I needed a shelter, were you there, were you
there?
When I needed a shelter, were you there?
And the creed and the colour and the name won't
matter,
Were you there?

When I needed a healer, were you there, were you
there?
When I needed a healer, were you there?
And the creed and the colour and the name won't
matter,
Were you there?

Wherever you travel, I'll be there, I'll be there,
Wherever you travel, I'll be there,
And the creed and the colour and the name won't
matter,
I'll be there.

Sydney Carter b.1915
(*100 Hymns for Today*)

Northern Ireland

I'm always very pleased whenever **Songs of Praise** comes
from Northern Ireland. Catholics and Protestants always
all take part together. Christians of all denominations are
extremely friendly with one another in Northern Ireland

– they are probably far more ecumenical (that's a good word, Thora!) than we are in the rest of Britain.

Those people who take part in **Songs of Praise** from Northern Ireland do a good job of reminding us that ninety-nine per cent of the population long for peace, and for the troubles to be over. Christians work together very hard to ensure that life in the towns and villages goes on peacefully and normally.

News and current affairs programmes on television only show us pictures of life when something violent and terrible has happened, so that a lot of us get the impression that the whole Province is one vast war zone. When you're watching **Songs of Praise** and **Praise Be!**, remember it's not only the friendlier and happier times, but also the more usual way of life in Northern Ireland that we are being shown, praise be!

Dear Lord, may the days of violence soon be over.

Now the Day is Over

Now the day is over,
Night is drawing nigh,
Shadows of the evening
Steal across the sky.

Now the darkness gathers,
Stars begin to peep,
Birds and beasts and flowers
Soon will be asleep.

Jesu, give the weary
Calm and sweet repose;

With thy tenderest blessing
May our eyelids close.

Grant to little children
Visions bright of Thee;
Guard the sailors tossing
On the deep blue sea.

Comfort every sufferer
Watching late in pain;
Those who plan some evil
From their sin restrain.

When the morning wakens,
Then may I arise
Pure, and fresh, and sinless
In Thy holy eyes.

Glory to the Father,
Glory to the Son,
And to Thee, blest Spirit,
Whilst all ages run.

S. Baring-Gould (1834–1924)

The Nun's Prayer

I don't know of any prayer that I've ever chosen to read
on **Praise Be!** that has had such a big response as this
twelfth-century nun's prayer.

Lord, Thou knowest better than I know myself
that I am growing older and will some day be old.

Keep me from the fatal habit of thinking I must say
something on every subject, and on every occasion.
Release me from craving to straighten out everybody's
   affairs.
Make me thoughtful, but not moody, helpful, but not
   bossy.
With my vast stores of wisdom,
it seems a pity not to use it all.
But Thou knowest, Lord, I want a few friends at the end.

Keep me reasonably sweet. I do not want to be a saint —
some of them are so hard to live with.
But a sour old person
is one of the crowning works of the Devil.

Keep my mind free from the recital of endless details;
give me wings to get to the point.
Seal my lips on my aches and pains.
They are increasing and love of rehearsing them
is becoming sweeter as the years go by.
I dare not ask for grace enough
to enjoy the tales of others' pains,
but help me to endure them with patience.

I dare not ask for improved memory
but for a growing humility,
and a lessening cocksureness when my memory
seems to clash with the memories of others.
Teach me the glorious lesson that occasionally
I may be mistaken.

Give me the ability to see good things
in unexpected places
and talents in unexpected people.
And give me, O Lord, the grace to tell them so.

                    Anon. Found in Rochester Cathedral

Old Age

"You are old, Father William,"
The young man said,
"And your hair has become very white,
And yet you incessantly stand on your head –
Do you think, at your age, it is right?"

"In my youth", Father William replied to his son,
"I feared it might injure the brain;
But now that I'm perfectly sure I have none,
Why, I do it again and again."

Lewis Carroll © 1925.

Old Age

The Nun's Prayer leads us neatly into O for Old Age. It can come as a fearful shock, the realization that you yourself are growing old. Other people are old, not you.

They say "You're as young as you feel" but that's part of the trouble. Most of us go on feeling about twenty-five long after they've handed us our bus passes. I've sometimes found myself addressing a gathering of people for some charity do, and telling them what a wonderful difference it would make to have – well, let's say a British Telecom Life-line – for "an old person". Even as I'm speaking the thought sometimes occurs to me "So why haven't Scotty and I got a Life-line?"

We all make jokes about being old age pensioners, expecting everyone to laugh with us. But one day their laugh doesn't sound quite right, so you take a long look at yourself in the mirror, and for a few awful moments, you feel very old indeed.

But I really don't think we should worry ourselves about growing older. Apart from a few extra aches and pains, growing old brings with it a lot of good things. Oh yes it does. You can speak your mind, for one thing. Even bank managers turn into young whipper-snappers. They say that when policemen start looking younger, that's the first sign of old age. So what does it mean when the Chelsea Pensioners are beginning to look quite boyish?

I think Robert Browning sums it all up for us:

> Grow old along with me
> The best is yet to be,
> The last of life, for which
> the first was made;
> Our times are in His hand
> Who saith, "A whole I planned,
> Youth shows but half: trust God:
> See all, be not afraid."
>
> Robert Browning (Rabbi Ben Ezra)

The Old Rugged Cross

Here is just one of several thousand letters I have received over the years, requesting this old favourite. It seems to be the one that keeps more people going than any other.

Dear Thora,
    It is like a rainbow shining when you are on.
    Well, I would like you to play '' The Old Rugged Cross''. You see, we lost my sister a few years ago, and the Sunday before she died on the Wednesday morning 6th February, I carried her into my bungalow. She was only little. But she was a wonderful person. She had been Blind through German Measles when she was seven. She was 77 when she died.
    She used to sing it at the Blind Socials. Well, that day she sang as if she was a young girl again.
    I am her sister, Kathleen. I shall be 80 in March. Would you play it in memory of my sister, Florence? Thank you very much indeed. God bless you.
    Love from Kathleen.
PS My Mother had 11 children, 7 still alive.

You almost seem to read the folk history of our whole nation in a letter like that, in just a few short sentences. My only regret is that I don't have enough time on **Praise Be!** to read out all the beautiful letters I receive, like Kathleen's.
    Each year I get several hundred letters asking for ''The Old Rugged Cross''. I think we must thank the Salvation Army for making it so beloved.

The Old Rugged Cross

On a hill far away stood an old rugged cross
The emblem of suffering and shame;
And I love that old cross, where the dearest and best
For a world of lost sinners was slain.

So I'll cherish the old rugged cross
'Til my trophies at last I lay down;
I will cling to the old cross
And exchange it some day for a crown.

Oh, the old rugged cross, so despised by the world,
Has a wondrous attraction for me;
For the dear Lamb of God left His glory above
To bear it to dark Calvary.

So I'll cherish the old rugged cross
'Til my trophies at last I lay down;
I will cling to the old cross
And exchange it some day for a crown.

To the old rugged cross I will ever be true
Its shame and reproach gladly bear;
Then He'll call me some day to my home far away
Where His glory for ever I'll share.

So I'll cherish the old rugged cross
'Til my trophies at last I lay down;
I will cling to the old cross
And exchange it some day for a crown.

The Rev. George Bennard ©1913
(© renewal 1941 The Rodeheaver Co.)

Onward Christian Soldiers

Luckily for me lots of people love my own favourite hymn, "Onward Christian Soldiers", so I get enough requests to justify including it most years!

I'm sure I must have mentioned on **Praise Be!** how my happiest memories of singing it are of when our grandchildren still *were* children, and we discovered it was the best way to keep them moving along when Scotty, Jan and I took them out for a walk. You know how children will lag behind – but no one lagged when we marched along in single file singing:

> Onward, Christian soldiers!
> Marching as to war,
> With the Cross of Jesus
> Going on before.
> Christ the royal Master
> Leads against the foe;
> Forward into battle,
> See, His banners go!
> Onward, Christian soldiers!
> Marching as to war,
> With the Cross of Jesus
> Going on before.
>
> Like a mighty army
> Moves the Church of God;
> Brothers, we are treading
> Where the saints have trod:
> We are not divided,
> All one body we,
> One in hope and doctrine,

One in charity.
Onward, Christian soldiers!
Marching as to war,
With the Cross of Jesus
Going on before.

Crowns and thrones may perish,
Kingdoms rise and wane,
But the Church of Jesus
Constant will remain:
Gates of hell can never
'Gainst that Church prevail;
We have Christ's own promise,
And that cannot fail.
Onward, Christian soldiers!
Marching as to war,
With the Cross of Jesus
Going on before.

Onward, then, ye people,
Join our happy throng,
Blend with ours your voices
In the triumph song:
Glory, laud, and honour
Unto Christ the King,
This through countless ages
Men and angels sing:
Onward, Christian soldiers!
Marching as to war,
With the Cross of Jesus
Going on before.

S. Baring-Gould (1834–1924)

Peter

"Thou art Peter, and upon this rock I will build my church;
and the gates of hell shall not prevail against it.'

Matthew 16:18 (AV)

Prayers

Everyone prays sometimes. Even non-believers. Rabbi Lionel Blue, who I so enjoyed talking to when he joined me on **Praise Be!** recently, tells this story in his wise and funny book *Bright Blue*:

A man fell over a precipice. As he fell, he managed to clutch on to the branch of a little tree which was growing out of the side of the cliff. As he hung there, he started to pray. "If there is anybody up there, please save me!"

A voice answered from heaven, saying "Fear not. I shall answer thy prayer.Just let go, and the palm of my hand will support thee and bring thee safely up."

There was a long pause. Then the man prayed again, saying: "Is there anybody else up there?"

If you believe in God, you probably try to pray regularly. My way of praying is to talk to the Lord as I would to a friend – well, He is a friend. I don't think

I'm always as good at listening to what's He's got to say to me as I should be, but I talk to Him every day.

Viewers often send me particular prayers which have helped them, and when there's time I read some of these out. Here are just a few which I have enjoyed reading.

Martha's Prayer

Lord, defend me from feeling hard-done by
when the chores seem endless.
Forgive me when I am bored by the constantly recurring
   need to think about food.
Teach me to organize myself in order not to be rushed
but never to be ruled by organization
and always to have time to listen.
Make me laugh, not swear,
when the milk boils over.
Preserve me from getting in a fuss
when the Grand-Joneses are coming to dinner.
Let me thank You daily for my home, for warmth and
   food,
and for my friends and family.
Lord, remind me often that
it takes Martha as well as Mary
to serve You perfectly.

Clemency Greatorix (Goudhurst) 1983

Prayer for Fighters

Lord, help me to remember
that nothing is going to happen today
that you and I together
can't handle!

Anon

The Dog's Prayer

O Lord of all creatures, grant that man, my master,
may be as faithful to other men as I am to him.

Make him as loving towards his family and friends
as I am loving to him.
Grant that he may guard with honesty the good things
with which Thou has endowed him
as honestly as I guard his.

Give him, O Lord, a happy and ready smile,
as happy and spontaneous as the wagging of my tail.
Make him as ready to show gratitude
as I am eager to lick his hand.
Give him patience as great as mine
when I await his return without complaining.
Grant him my courage and my readiness
to sacrifice all for him, even my life.
May he possess my youthful spirit and joy of thought.

O Lord of all creatures, as I am in truth only a dog,
may my master always be truly a man.

Pero Scanziani

Little Girl's Prayer

God bless Mummy, and Daddy, my brother Tommy,
  my best friend Susan.
God bless Grannie and all my friends at Brownies.
And God, please take care of Yourself –
  because if anything happens to You –
  we've had it!

Anon

Psalms

The Psalms are prayers which we can either say or sing.
In Scotland they have developed the tradition of the
metrical psalm, which can be sung to their lovely Gaelic
hymn tunes that are so simple and appealing. Somehow
the metric form of the words makes them easier to
remember, too. Here's one I am often asked for on **Praise
Be!**

Psalm 121 (metric version)

I to the hills will lift mine eyes,
from whence doth come mine aid.
My safety cometh from the Lord,
who heav'n and earth hath made.
Thy foot He'll not let slide, nor will

He slumber that thee keeps.
Behold, He that keeps Israel,
He slumbers not, nor sleeps.
The Lord thee keeps, the Lord thy shade
on thy right hand doth stay;
The moon by night Thee shall not smite,
nor yet the sun by day.
The Lord shall keep thy soul; He shall
preserve thee from all ill.
Henceforth thy going out and in
God keep for ever will.

Poems

As well as prayers, I also receive hundreds of poems which viewers have written themselves, or found somewhere, and realized that I too would enjoy them. I have a lot of fun reading them, and am sorry that I can usually only manage to include one or two each year in the series. I am grateful to Mrs Regina Massey of Letchworth for the following one, which she tells me she extorted from her Senior Over 60 club. (I say, Regina! I wonder what the Junior Over 60 club is like!)

Sounds Familiar

Just a line to say I'm living –
That I'm not among the dead,

Though I'm getting more forgetful
And mixed up in the head.
I've got used to my arthritis
To my dentures I'm resigned,
I can cope with my bi-focals,
But – ye gods – I miss my mind!'
Sometimes I can't remember
When I'm standing by the stair,
If I'm going up for something
Or have just come down from there.
And before the fridge so often
My mind is full of doubt:
Now did I put some food away –
Or have I come to take some out?
So, remember, I do love you,
And wish that you lived near.
And now it's time to post this
And say goodbye, my dear.

At last I stand beside the postbox
And my face – I'm sure it's red –
Instead of posting this to you,
I've opened it instead!

                                            Anon

After the programme in which I read the following poem,
I received hundreds of requests for copies. It was written
by Enrolled Nurse Kathy Doyle, when she was working
at the Infirmary of the Royal Hospital, Chelsea, nursing
the Chelsea Pensioners.

Nursing the Elderly

He was a child before we were born –
Now he is helpless, old and forlorn.
He was a husband long years ago,
He walked with his wife, their cheeks all aglow.
His wife was a mother; she had babes at her breast,
Caring for others, and giving her best.
He was a man, salute him for this,
Now he is withered, and harder to kiss.
Speak to him gently, and nurse him with pride,
Now, as he waits to sail with the tide.
Ours are the last hands he'll ever hold.
Let him know love, now he is old.

Kathy Doyle

Another of my favourite hymns is sometimes our
"theme" music for **Praise Be!** – with its joyful chorus
of Praise the Lord!

Praise the Lord (To God be the glory!)

To God be the glory! Great things He hath done.
So loved He the world that He gave us His son;
Who yielded His life, an atonement for sin,
And opened the life gate that all may go in.

Praise the Lord! Praise the Lord!
Let the earth hear His voice!

Praise the Lord! Praise the Lord!
Let the people rejoice!
O come to the Father, through Jesus the Son;
And give Him the glory! Great things He hath done!

O perfect redemption, the purchase of blood!
To every believer the promise of God;
The vilest offender who truly believes,
That moment from Jesus a pardon receives.

Great things He hath taught us, great things He hath
  done,
And great our rejoicing through Jesus the Son:
But purer, and higher, and greater will be
Our wonder, our rapture, when Jesus we see.

Praise the Lord! Praise the Lord!
Let the earth hear His voice.
Praise the Lord! Praise the Lord!
Let the people rejoice.
O come to the Father, through Jesus the Son;
And give Him the glory. Great things He hath done!

                    Frances van Alstyne (1820–1915)

Drop thy still dews of quietness
'Til all our strivings cease

J. G. Whittier (1807–1892)

Quakers

There could hardly be a greater contrast to the exuberance and excitement of a Pentecostal service, or the Gospel Singers' **Songs of Praise** from Southwark Cathedral, which I described under G, with everyone singing, dancing, stamping, clapping, and shouting out "Allelujah! Praise the Lord!", than the deep, meditative quiet of Quaker worship, in which the Friends gather together in silence for spiritual converse with God.

The Friends don't sing hymns as part of their services, but J. G. Whittier, the New England poet who wrote "Dear Lord and Father of Mankind", which I've quoted above (and written out in full, under D), was himself a Quaker. He was an interesting man, John Whittier. He was brought up in a Quaker household, on a farm in Massachusetts. When he was a boy, his sister sent one of his poems to William Lloyd Garrison, who was editor of the Free Press. Garrison was so impressed, he rode over to meet the lad, and tried to persuade his father to give him a good education, so that he could become a writer. His father replied "Poetry will not give him bread".

Later, John Whittier joined Garrison in the fight against slavery, and became the poet of the struggle. He wrote several hymns, including "O brother man, fold to thy heart thy brother", but "Dear Lord and Father of Mankind" is by far the best known.

I often get requests from Quakers for hymns on **Praise Be!**, but unfortunately, I can't think of a suitable one beginning with a Q! Instead, here is the quiet, prayerful one from the Sarum Primer, which so many of us love for its simplicity and beauty.

God Be in My Head

God be in my head,
And in my understanding;
God be in my eyes,
And in my looking;
God be in my mouth,
And in my speaking;
God be in my heart,
And in my thinking;
God be at my end,
And at my departing.

after R. Pynson (1514)

Questions

The question I get asked most frequently is "Why didn't you play my hymn?"!

I'll never forget one occasion when I was with Yorkshire Television filming **In Loving Memory**, and that clever director, Ronnie Baxter, had set up a "shot" which would show the whole of the beautiful old Yorkshire village with its steeply sloping cobbled street. There were about sixty "extras" involved, because we were filming Billy, my nephew's, funeral (although he wasn't really dead) and everyone had turned out to pay their respects. Billy's friend, Ernie, was driving the hearse (carrying an empty coffin with a brown bowler on the top!), and I followed behind in the first car.

Right! Ronnie Baxter and the crew were set up half a mile away to film the whole sequence. Everything was going well, the sun was doing a perfect job of setting in a cloudless sky, the cortege stopped so that I could get out to say my line to one of the "extras" lining the village street, when all of a sudden a woman who'd been standing with a group of spectators watching the filming, stepped forward right into the middle of the "shot". She was wearing a bright red trouser suit, and she had a fag jutting straight out from her mouth while she spoke. She started saying "You never played my hymn!" I heard the director shout out "Cut!", and I said to her, "I'm sorry, but you're right in the middle of the shot. Could you just wait until we've finished filming, and I'll talk to you then?"

As soon as we finished, she came straight back, another fag on the go, "Well, you never played my hymn. It was my favourite. And it was my mother's favourite, and you never played it!''

I said to her, ''I'm most awfully sorry. I can't always manage to include everybody's choice. What hymn was it?''

''It was my mother's favourite, and my favourite, and you never . . . what?''

''What hymn was it?''

''Oh! Well, I can't just think . . .'' After all that, she'd forgotten what her favourite hymn was!

I do try very hard to fit in as many people's requests as possible. I think that sometimes when people tell me I didn't play their hymn, perhaps what they've noticed is that I didn't read out their name. But as I so often say on the programme, if I mentioned everybody's names, there'd be no time for any hymns at all!

Another very commonly asked question is ''Why can't we have the words on the screen for all the hymns?'' Yes! I know! I *know*! That's just what you wanted to ask me, too, isn't it? (Oh yes, just because you're reading my book, doesn't mean I can't read your mind! To say nothing of the hundreds of letters you've all written asking me the same question.)

Well, in the first place, it's not up to me. I present the programmes, but there's a whole team at the BBC of people who are in charge of the production. However, I do know the reasons, or some of them.

For the first twenty years or so of **Songs of Praise** it wasn't possible to put the words on the screen. Or it may just about have been technically possible, but it would have been very difficult, expensive and time-consuming, and the budget wouldn't have allowed it.

Then, over the years, the producers began to realize that one of the main strengths of the programme, and why it was so popular, was not just the sound of familiar, well-loved hymns being sung, but it was the faith which showed on the faces of the people singing, and the interest and beauty of seeing all the different churches, chapels and cathedrals each week.

So even though it has become an easier matter to put the words up over the pictures, they are still reluctant to do it.

It is true, you know, that once the words go up on the screen, your eye finds it very difficult to take in anything else. You almost might as well have a black background, and save the expense and bother of filming all the beautiful churches full of people singing their hearts out! That's what they fear, anyway.

However, because so many people have continued to press for the words, three things have happened. The first is that all the programmes are Ceefaxed (you may remember seeing me, one year, visit the girls at Ceefax, and having a go at putting the words up to a hymn myself. Oh I did enjoy myself!) This means that anyone with a Ceefax set can have the words if they want to. The second thing they've done is to put the words up on all the hymns for the repeat showing of the programmes the next day on BBC 2. The third thing is my own contribution, which is to plead each year to be allowed to put the words up for at least one hymn a week, so that the **Praise Be!** viewers and I can all have a good sing together.

So now you know as much as I do!

"A number of buttons have been found among the coins in recent collections. In future, please:
 'Rend your hearts, and not your garments.' "

quoted in *Ripon Bits and Pieces*

Rules

I expect most of us live by all sorts of unwritten rules. I know I do. A lot of mine are to do with everyday routines. We never leave the house, for instance, without going through our little list of procedures, which are mainly to do with security, but also we'd never go out leaving washing up undone in the bowl, or the place untidy, the beds unmade. (Ooh, don't I sound like Mrs Perfect! But you know I don't mean it like that.)

When we were making a special **Praise Be!** programme to mark the Wesleys' bi-centenary in 1988, I came across this, which John Wesley made his own special rule for living:

> Do all the good you can
> By all the means you can
> In all the ways you can
> At all the times you can
> To all the people you can
> As long as you can.

John Wesley

Religious communities of nuns and monks always live by a Rule, with a capital R, which sets out how to live the religious life the way that their founders saw it, sometimes many centuries ago. Benedictines, for example, to this day live by the Rule written by St Benedict for his monks living in Italy in the sixth century.

Doesn't that seem strange? I was wondering, whatever could St Benedict possibly have had to say that would be of use to anyone today? But when you come to think of it, all Christians are trying to live by the rule of the gospels. And the words of Jesus are as fresh today as if He were speaking especially to us.

I've seen part of St Benedict's Rule – not all of it, of course – but even from the little bits I read, I would think that it would help anyone, not just a monk or a nun, but even an ordinary Christian like you and me, and you don't even need to be a scholar. Because it's nearly all about looking for, and finding, Jesus in ordinary, everyday things, like when you're tired, and you make a cup of tea, and feel thankful to sit down and enjoy it. Here are just one or two short pieces from the Rule, so you can see what I mean:

In the introduction to his Rule, St Benedict wrote:

The Lord has Himself given us the time and space necessary to learn
and put into practice the service of love that He continues to teach us.
In this school of His let us hope that following faithfully His instructions.
nothing distasteful nor burdensome will be demanded of us,

but if it has to be so in order to overcome our egoism
and lead us into the depths of true love,
let us not become disheartened, nor frightened
and so ignore the narrow path in spite of its tight
   entrance –
that path which leads directly to the fullness of life.

Trs. Ambrose Wathen (Cistercian Studies 1980, XV p.106)

The utensils required for the kitchen service are to be
   washed and returned to the cellarer.

(Rule 35: 20)

(In our house, Scotty is the cellarer, and I'm the one who
washes the utensils required for the kitchen service!)

Never give a hollow greeting of peace
or turn away when someone needs your love.

(Rule 4: 25–6)

We believe that the Divine Presence is everywhere, and
   that in every place the eye of the Lord is watching.

(Rule of St Benedict: 19:1)

Rules are there to help us, but if you're anything like me
you won't always be Mrs Perfect, or able to stick to them.
But even if we despair of ourselves sometimes, our
favourite hymns remind us that we need never despair
of God's love and forgiveness.

Rock of Ages

Rock of ages, cleft for me,
Let me hide myself in Thee;
Let the water and the blood,
From Thy riven side which flowed,
Be of sin the double cure:
Cleanse me from its guilt and power.

Not the labours of my hands
Can fulfil Thy law's demands;
Could my zeal no respite know,
Could my tears for ever flow,
All for sin could not atone:
Thou must save, and Thou alone.

Nothing in my hand I bring,
Simply to Thy Cross I cling;
naked, come to Thee for dress;
Helpless, look to Thee for grace;
Foul, I to the fountain fly;
Wash me, Saviour, or I die.

While I draw this fleeting breath,
When my eyelids close in death,
When I soar through tracts unknown,
See Thee on Thy judgement throne;
Rock of ages, cleft for me,
Let me hide myself in Thee.

Augustus Toplady (1740–1778)

Remembrance

Another group of people for whom rules and discipline are very important, are the Services. The dedicated men and women of our armed forces demonstrate a way of life which is organized, disciplined, unselfish and useful.

Some very peace-minded people, including some Christians, are surprised by the number of Christian hymns which use military expressions: hymns like my own favourite, "Onward, Christian Soldiers"; "Stand up, stand up for Jesus"; "Soldiers of Christ arise"; "Soldiers, who are Christ's below"; "Jerusalem"; "Fight the good Fight" – Oh, I expect you can think of many more besides. I don't personally find it surprising at all. You introduce me to any parish church in Britain that is thriving, and gives caring service to the community round about, and I'm sure I'll be able to come and point out to you a large number of both active and retired military folk among the congregation.

Until a few years ago, the letters I received asking for the hymns we sing on Remembrance Sunday were nearly all from the families of men and women who had lost their lives in the First and Second World Wars, and who remembered them with pride. Now, of course, we have the Falklands War to remember too.

Rejoice, O Land

Rejoice, O land, in God thy might;
His will obey, Him serve aright;
For thee the saints uplift their voice:
Fear not, O land, in God rejoice.

Glad shalt thou be, with blessing crowned,
With joy and peace thou shalt abound;
Yea, love with thee shall make His home
Until thou see God's kingdom come.

He shall forgive thy sins untold:
Remember thou His love of old;
Walk in His way, His word adore,
And keep His truth for evermore.

Yattendon Hymnal

Seven days without God
make one WEAK!

The Seven Last Words of the Church:
"We never did it that way before."

Sixpence

Go on! You can't fool me! Of course you can remember what a sixpence is! This story is about a lesson my mother taught me that has stood me in good stead all my life.

More than fifty years ago Scotty and I returned home from our honeymoon, on a train from Forfar that arrived in Morecambe around lunchtime. Instead of making straight for our own new home, "Prompt Corner", we went first to number 6, Cheapside. Naturally, I was longing to see the family and tell them all about my honeymoon, and also, to be honest, as it was lunchtime, I hoped we would get some of my mother's home cooking.

The wonderful smell of lamb and mint sauce wafted up our noses as we opened the front door. After loving hugs all round, my mother said that they had already eaten. "We had lamb chops, and I would have prepared some extra if I'd known you were coming. But there are plenty of new potatoes left, and mint sauce. I know, why don't you nip round to the butcher's and get a couple of lamb chops? You can grill them here, and we can hear all your news.''

Quite simple and straightforward, except that she didn't know that the newlyweds had only three shillings and eightpence between them to last until Friday (and it was only Monday). Three shillings and eightpence? Get away with you. (Well, if you really must know, just under twenty pence. Gracious!) Never mind. I bought two lovely chops for tenpence (i.e. 4 pence. Well, I am talking ancient history!) reducing the housekeeping cash to two shillings and tenpence.

There was apple pie and custard on the table, so after we had eaten the chops I said to Scotty, ''Apple pie and custard, love?'' and as I cut him a generous wedge my mother said, ''It's threepence a portion.'' I nearly dropped the plate on his lap. Then I started to laugh, and said in a very assured way, ''Yes, I'm sure it is!'' ''But it *is*'' protested my mother very seriously. ''And two portions will be sixpence.''

I gave her sixpence, and didn't enjoy my three-pennyworth at all. My own, generous mother, who gave everybody everything, charging *me*, her own daughter, threepence a portion for apple pie and custard!

As we walked to our new home, poor Scotty had to listen to me exclaiming and moaning all the way, ''I'd never have believed it! My own mother! I'd never have believed it!''

Of course, the excitement of walking in to ''Prompt Corner'' as man and wife put it all out of our minds for a while. Scotty had to go to work that evening at the Winter Gardens. I went to meet him afterwards, and we called in again at 6, Cheapside to say ''Goodnight, God bless'' as it was on our way home.

In the centre of the dining table were two large plate pies, a savoury one and an apple one. My mother started to wrap them in greaseproof paper, and burst out laughing as she did so. I pretended I didn't see the joke, but she had a very infectious laugh, and soon Scotty started laughing too.

"It was worth it, to see your face at lunch time", my mother explained.

"Well, there was no need to charge me!" I retorted indignantly.

"Oh yes there was. You're a married woman now, and you'll have to learn to make your money spin out . . . If you want anything badly enough and can't afford it, you'll just have to wait until you've saved up for it."

Well, she was right about that, and how often Scotty and I have saved for some special item, enjoying the anticipation of buying it as much as the thing itself. But another thing she taught me was that love doesn't always or only come in the form of hugs and kisses. It sometimes comes in the form of a firm rebuke.

When we got home, we unwrapped the pies to discover that the apple one had a centre decoration. My sixpence! I wish I could end by saying that "and I still have that sixpence to this very day." But unfortunately it was gone before the end of that same week!

I've included this less well-known hymn, because the words are about a wonderful moment, that can catch you quite by surprise, when you suddenly understand how much God really loves you. Not all of *His* loving lessons come through hugs and kisses either!

Sometimes a Light Surprises

Sometimes a light surprises
The Christian while he sings:
It is the Lord who rises
With healing in His wings;
When comforts are declining,
He grants the soul again
A season of clear shining
To cheer it after rain.

In holy contemplation
We sweetly then pursue
The theme of God's salvation,
And find it ever new:
Set free from present sorrow,
We cheerfully can say,
E'en let the unknown morrow
Bring with it what it may.

It can bring with it nothing
But He will bear us through;
Who gives the lilies clothing
Will clothe His people too:
Beneath the spreading heavens
No creature but is fed;

And He who feeds the ravens
Will give His children bread.

Though vine nor fig-tree neither
Their wonted fruit should bear,
Though all the fields should wither,
Nor flocks nor herds be there;
Yet, God the same abiding,
His praise shall tune my voice;
For, while in Him confiding,
I cannot but rejoice.

William Cowper (1731–1800)

Salvation Army

Another television character I very much enjoyed playing
was Captain Emily Ridley in the series **Allelujah!** which,
like **In Loving Memory**, was written by Dick Sharples.
I liked Captain Emily. She wasn't one of life's successes,
in fact she was a failure. Nothing ever went right for her,
she was accident prone and she'd really only been put
in charge of this Salvation Army Citadel to keep her out
of harm's way. It was one that had practically closed
down, no one went there any more, and it was a hopeless
task.

She herself, of course, never realized this, and regarded
it as the greatest honour to have been put in charge of
her own Citadel. Helped by the faithful Alice Meredith,
delightfully played by Patsy Rowlands, she set about,
week after week, trying to go about doing good, and
gathering together a congregation and a band.

Emily was an interesting character, an innocent who talked to the Lord, rather in the way I do myself, and told Him all her problems. And because the Lord doesn't seem to mind as much as we do about success and failure, a lot of what she set out to do, guided by her friend the Lord, began very well. But because she was this hopeless sort of person, she usually managed to mess it all up again by the end.

It was fun playing a Salvation Army Captain, I loved the uniform, and it introduced me to Rob Garrod, a real Salvation Army Captain, who acted as consultant to the programme, and has become a great friend. I've always loved the Salvation Army, of course, and am a great admirer of all the wonderful work they do. Every day, all over the world, thousands of people turn to the Salvation Army for help when they are in too much trouble to help themselves.

Their bands and songsters have made a great contribution to church music, too. I've never forgotten that band at Morecambe who played down our street every Christmas, and down on the beach during the summer. There's something very haunting about the sound of cornets playing out in the open air, isn't there?

In her own funny way Captain Emily Ridley was one of God's saints, and the many thousands of real Salvation Army officers, with all their kindness – and great competence! – certainly are.

For All the Saints

For all the saints who from their labours rest,
Who Thee by faith before the world confessed,
Thy name, O Jesu, be for ever blest.
        Alleluia!

Thou wast their rock, their fortress, and their might;
Thou, Lord, their captain in the well-fought fight;
Thou, in the darkness, still their one true Light.
        Alleluia!

O may Thy soldiers, faithful, true, and bold,
Fight as the saints who nobly fought of old,
And win, with them, the victor's crown of gold.
        Alleluia!

O blest communion, fellowship divine!
We feebly struggle, they in glory shine;
Yet all are one in Thee, for all are Thine.
        Alleluia!

And when the strife is fierce, the warfare long,
Steals on the ear the distant triumph-song,
And hearts are brave again and arms are strong.
        Alluluia!

The golden evening brightens in the west;
Soon, soon to faithful warriors comes their rest;
Sweet is the calm of Paradise the blest.
        Alluluia!

But lo, there breaks a yet more glorious day;
The saints triumphant rise in bright array:
The King of Glory passes on His way.
        Alleluia!

From earth's wide bounds, from ocean's farthest coast,
Through gates of pearl streams in the countless host,
Singing to Father, Son and Holy Ghost.
                    Alleluia!

The loss of gold is great
The loss of time is more
But losing Christ is such a loss
As no man can restore.

> (inscription on Sunderland
> ware bowl)

Today's mighty oak is yesterday's little nut
that held its ground. . . . .

The Tapestry

On the very first series of **Praise Be!** I had the help and
advice of a very charming Methodist Minister, called the
Rev. Frank Pagden, and I always remember him saying
that life was like a piece of tapestry: when you look at
the back, all you can see are a mass of loose ends, and
lumps and tangled up patches of wool, and you can't
make out the pattern of it. Only when you turn the
tapestry over to look at the right side can you see what
the picture is. We are always looking at our own lives
from the wrong side of the tapestry, so we can't
understand the purpose of it, and sometimes, when
we're feeling very low, we think there isn't any purpose
at all. But God is looking at the right side of the tapestry.

I like that idea, don't you? I talked about it on the

programme fourteen years ago. Ever since then, though, this tapestry story has been cropping up in all sorts of places, and there are always new people who read about it or hear it for the first time, and then they think "Oh this is good. I'll send it off to Thora, and she can use it on **Praise Be!**"

The hymn I introduced with this story of the tapestry, and which followed on quite naturally, I felt, was "Through all the changing scenes of life".

Through all the Changing Scenes of Life

Through all the changing scenes of life,
In trouble and in joy,
The praises of my God shall still
My heart and tongue employ.

O magnify the Lord with me,
With me exalt His name;
When in distress to Him I called,
He to my rescue came.

The hosts of God encamp around
The dwellings of the just;
Deliverance He affords to all
Who on His succour trust.

O make but trial of His love:
Experience will decide
How blest are they, and only they,
Who in His truth confide.

Fear Him, ye saints, and you will then
Have nothing else to fear;
Make you His service your delight,
Your wants shall be His care.

To Father, Son and Holy Ghost,
The God whom we adore
Be glory, as it was is now,
And shall be evermore.

N. Tate (1652–1715)
and N. Brady (1659–1726)

Time

Anyone who has ever worked with me will tell you, Thora is never late. Early – often. Very early – sometimes. But never late. I think it's extremely important, if a group of people have agreed to meet together at a certain time, as you do if you're rehearsing a play in the theatre, for example, or making a television programme, that everyone gets there *on time*. You may arrive only one minute late, but you could be keeping perhaps thirty other people waiting for that one minute, so really you should think of yourself as being 30 minutes late. My dad pointed that out to me many years ago, and I've never forgotten.

Time is very precious, and shouldn't be wasted, even by young people who think they've got far more of it than they need.

One of my most faithful and regular correspondents over the years has been Mrs Edna Cattermole, from New

Longton, near Preston. Last year Edna sent me these lines
about time, that are written on the clock in Chester
Cathedral (I've seen them there myself, too):

Time

When as a child I laughed and wept –
Time crept
When as a youth I waxed more bold –
Time strolled
When I became a full grown man –
Time ran
When older still I grew –
Time flew
Soon I shall find in passing on –
Time gone
O Christ wilt Thou have saved me then –
Amen.

Earlier in the day than **Praise Be!** the BBC's worship
programme goes out every Sunday morning from a
different person's home. It's called **This is the Day**, from
Psalm 118:

This is the day which the Lord hath made; we will
rejoice and be glad in it,

and a popular folk hymn has also been written around
the same words:

This is the Day

This is the day, this is the day
That the Lord has made, that the Lord has made.
We will rejoice, we will rejoice
And be glad in it, and be glad in it.
This is the day that the Lord has made
We will rejoice and be glad in it
This is the day, this is the day
That the Lord has made.

This is the day, this is the day
When He rose again, when He rose again
We will rejoice, we will rejoice
And be glad in it, and be glad in it.
This is the day that the Lord has made
We will rejoice and be glad in it
This is the day, this is the day
When He rose again.

This is the day, this is the day
When the Spirit came, when the Spirit came
We will rejoice, we will rejoice
And be glad in it, and be glad in it.
This is the day that the Lord has made
We will rejoice and be glad in it
This is the day, this is the day
When the Spirit came.

Thank You

T is for Thank you. The main reason for compiling this little book has been to thank all the people who each year on **Praise Be!** send me their letters and so often include delightful prayers and verses, which I can then read out and share with the millions of people who watch the programme.

Sometimes they also enclose money, which they ask me to give to my favourite charity. The money they send, and the proceeds of this book, all go into the Thora Hird Charitable Trust, of which Scotty, Jan and I are joint Trustees. The Trust sends money to different charities as we hear about their needs. But please don't send me money! It's much better for you to give your own money, with your love, to people who need your help.

I also want to thank all the contributors to church magazines whose items I read out and have used here. And the many anonymous authors of the Wayside Pulpit notices outside churches, which cause Scotty so much grief and me so much pleasure!

What is missing from this CH..CH?

Answer: U R!

Universe

When I was very little and first learned to write my own name and address, I used to put this on all my personal possessions:

> Thora Hird
> 6 Cheapside
> Morecambe
> Lancashire
> England
> Europe
> The World

and I might have added:

> The Universe!

I'd grown out of it by the time I was nine, but I'm thinking of taking it up again! I don't think it hurts to remember that however proud we may be of our own little space, our home and garden and neighbourhood, we should also be proud to be a tiny part of the entire created universe. I'm sure you must have come across these beautiful lines by the Indiana poet and philosopher, Max Ehrmann:

Desiderata

Go placidly amid the noise and the haste, and remember what peace there may be in silence. As far as possible, without surrender, be on good terms with all persons. Speak your truth quietly and clearly; and listen to others, even to the dull and ignorant; they too have their story.

Avoid loud and aggressive persons; they are vexatious to the spirit. If you compare yourself with others, you may become vain or bitter, for always there will be greater and lesser persons than yourself.

Enjoy your achievements as well as your plans. Keep interested in your own career, however humble; it is a real possession in the changing fortunes of time.

Exercise caution in your business affairs, for the world is full of trickery. But let this not blind you to what virtue there is; many persons strive for high ideals, and everywhere life is full of heroism.

Be yourself. Especially do not feign affection. Neither be cynical about love; for in the face of all aridity and disenchantment, it is as perennial as the grass. Take kindly the counsel of the years, gracefully surrendering the things of youth. Nurture strength of spirit to shield you in sudden misfortune. But do not distress yourself with dark imaginings. Many fears are born of fatigue and loneliness. Beyond a wholesome discipline, be gentle with yourself.

You are a child of the universe no less than the trees and the stars; you have a right to be here. And whether or not it is clear to you, no doubt the universe is unfolding as it should. Therefore, be at peace with God, whatever you conceive Him to be.

And whatever your labours and aspirations, in the noisy confusion of life, keep peace in your soul. With all its sham, drudgery and broken dreams, it is still a beautiful world. Be cheerful. Strive to be happy.

© 1927 Max Ehrmann
(Copyright renewed 1954 by Bertha K. Ehrmann)

Wise words, don't you agree?

Unto Us a Boy is Born

Unto us a boy is born,
King of all creation.
Came he to a world forlorn
The Lord of every nation.

Fifteenth-Century Carol

As I have mentioned, some unknown band of bell-ringers from St Lawrence's Parish Church in Morecambe were good enough to ring in my birth one Sunday morning on 28th May (even though I was a Methodist!), and I now have to thank the bell-ringers once again, for providing me with their fine hymn!

Unchanging God

Unchanging God, who livest
Enthroned in realms on high,
To men the power Thou givest
Thy name to magnify.
We raise the bells for ringing
With ready mind and will,
And come before Thee, bringing
our hearts, our strength, our skill.

We call, from tower and steeple,
Upon the day of days,
All faithful Christian people
To worship, prayer, and praise;
We ring with joyous gladness
When man and wife are blessed;
We peal in muffled sadness
For loved ones laid to rest.

By union free and willing
The work of God is done;
Our Master's prayer fulfilling,
We would in Him be one:
One, as the Church our Mother
Would have her children stand,

Befriending one another,
A strong and steadfast band.

Our lives, like bells, while changing,
An ordered course pursue;
Through joys and sorrows ranging
May all those lives ring true.
May we, by Christ forgiven
Our faults and failures past,
Attain our place in heaven,
Called home to rest at last.

H. C. Wilder
(Hymns Ancient & Modern)

Vicars

If you are unhappy with your vicar, simply have your churchwardens send a copy of this letter to six other churches who are also tired of their vicar.

Then bundle up your vicar and send him to the church at the top of the list in the letter.

Within a week you will receive 16,435 vicars – and one of them should be all right!

Have faith in this chain letter for vicars. Do not break the chain. One church did, and got their old vicar back!

(from a Salisbury Theological College leaflet)

Vocations

We would never let anything like that happen to our vicar! We all love him far too much. You might remember the Rev. Roger Dalling, from the little church in our village, because he's been with me on **Praise Be!** and so has Canon Bill Peters, who's the sort of boss vicar – or is he a rector? Anyway, he's Top Dog-collar round our way! We're always saying how lucky we are, doubly lucky, having two real smashers to look after us, because they are both such interesting men.

You can always tell if someone has a vocation. It means having a calling, and there's the world of difference between someone who just does their work for the money, and someone who has a calling. You only have to watch them at work for a few moments, you can see it in their faces. They get a sort of intense, lost to the world look, and they become completely absorbed in what they are doing.

I don't only mean vicars. Artists and musicians can have a vocation, so can cooks, so can mothers and housewives, nurses and prime ministers, computer operators, actors, house-painters and shorthand typists.

If you're that sort of person, do be careful. If your work takes you over too much, you can become exhausted, and then you might find yourself neglecting other parts of your life which are just as important. I mean your family and your home life, and your friends. You need them, and they need you, so you must keep some of your time and attention for them.

Loving your work isn't enough, even if you do have a vocation. We must love one another. There, and I said I wasn't going to preach to you! Never mind. End of sermon!

Veni, Creator Spiritus

Listen, it's not just me telling you that you need to rest as well as to work hard – some of our favourite hymns are telling you the same thing!

I Heard the Voice of Jesus Say

I heard the voice of Jesus say:
Come unto Me and rest;
Lay down, thou weary one, lay down
Thy head upon My breast!'
I came to Jesus as I was,
Weary, and worn, and sad;
I found in Him a resting place,
And He has made me glad.

I heard the voice of Jesus say:
"Behold, I freely give
The living water; thirsty one,
Stoop down and drink, and live!"
I came to Jesus, and I drank
Of that life-giving stream;
My thirst was quenched, my soul revived,
And now I live in Him.

I heard the voice of Jesus say:
"I am this dark world's light;
Look unto Me, thy morn shall rise,
And all thy day be bright!"
I looked to Jesus, and I found
In Him my star, my sun;
And that light of life I'll walk
Till travelling days are done.

Horatius Bonar (1808–1889)

Visitors

Roger, our vicar I was just telling you about, is especially good at talking to children. He holds them (and us!) spellbound with his stories. I remember one year he was talking about the journey of the Three Wise Men, and he wanted the children to picture it. He began by saying: "If Jesus had been born in one of the fields round our village, then Herod's palace would have been at Lewes. So after they left Herod, the Three Wise Men would have had to come across the Downs. Then where? Over that river at the bottom, wouldn't they, then down through the fields of the farm by the church, then another half a mile along the road to the Flying Fish – which instead of a car park would have had a yard full of animals round the back, and the stable where Mary and Joseph had to stay while Jesus was born." The children listened to him – you could have heard a pin drop. He has this story-teller's gift, you know.

If the Three Wise Men did ever happen to come through our village, I'd like to think that they'd call in at the church, have a look round and sign our visitors' book. It's a lovely little church, and you'd be amazed from how far and wide visitors do come.

There are thousands of old, sometimes *very* ancient, parish churches all over Great Britain, and you can have a fascinating time reading through all the names, places and comments in the visitors' books, left by strangers who have passed through and looked around between one Sunday and the next. Some of them will have said their prayers there, while you were away working; perhaps they were kneeling in "your" pew!

Even in our little village, we get visitors from all over

the world, especially from America, as well as from all parts of Britain. Sometimes they just put ''peaceful'' in the comments column. I reckon in today's busy world, that's high praise!

You may not know this hymn for children if you didn't go to a Methodist Sunday School. Yes, I know it doesn't begin with a V, but it is about Villages, and the Three Wise Men, and they were Visitors, weren't they?

Wise Men Seeking Jesus

Wise men seeking Jesus,
Travelled from afar,
Guided on their journey
By a beauteous star.

But if we desire Him,
He is close at hand;
For our native country
Is our Holy Land.

Prayerful souls may find Him
By our quiet lakes,
Meet Him on our hillsides
When the morning breaks.

In our fertile cornfields
While the sheaves are bound
In our busy markets,
Jesus may be found.

Fishermen talk with Him
By the great North Sea,

As the first disciples
Did in Galilee.

Every peaceful village
In our land might be
Made by Jesu's presence
Like sweet Bethany.

He is more than near us,
If we love Him well;
For He seeketh ever
In our hearts to dwell.

James Thomas East
(1860–1937)

Weather

"There's no such thing as bad weather. Only wrong clothes!"

Sigmund Freud

O western wind, when wilt thou blow,
That the small rain down shall rain
Christ, that my love were in my arms
And I in my bed again!

Anon

Worldwide Witness

It's been very exciting over the last few years, receiving more and more letters for **Praise Be!** from abroad. I've received many very charming letters from people all over the world, and especially from Holland. Here are just two of many which arrived from Voorburg and Rotterdam last year:

Dear Thora,
I am a woman of 70 years old, and I am sure that my English is not so good, but I hope that you can read this letter a little bit.
There is so many sadness in our lives, and

sometimes we feel so lonely, but two years ago, we
have a holiday in Benidorm, and we met an English
woman. She lay in Hospital for a few weeks, and
I visited her, and she told us about your nice
programme **Praise Be!**

She invited us to come to Sheffield, and so we do,
and we have a nice time. Thanks to Ivy and Cliff
Smith for the warm hospitality, and thanks to you
Thora Hird. May God bless all of you.
Mrs and Mr Kuyt Harteveld
Voorburg

Dear Mrs Hird,
Since some years we listen to the **Songs of Praise**
and **Praise Be!** We enjoy it very much.

The Christian Communion is so international and
we are happy that we know that God's Holy Ghost
is working all over the world.

The songs you sing are so nice, and the melodies.
Beautiful. Sometimes I play them on the organ in
the church.

We visited England several times, and I must say
we feel so at home. The green pastures and the
trees, the hills, the little villages with the old
churches . . . We always visit a church on Sunday.
And we talk with all the people. Sometimes we have
the Lord's Supper. And during the services, we feel
united in the belief that God loves us all so much.

Many people in Holland are listening to your
programme. Proceed and be a blessing for many
Christians and men and women who don't know
yet Jesus Christ.
Wessel Kaat
Rotterdam

You see! All the world will soon be joining us for **Praise Be!**

Say what you will about the bad effects of watching television (and I know some people are very critical of television, although I am not one of them), one of the good things it does is to bring into our homes news and pictures of people who live in every corner of the world, and to take our news to them.

Apart from the pleasure of being joined by our neighbours in Holland, Belgium and France for **Praise Be!**, there are also the problems and difficulties in other countries which we can learn about and sometimes be of assistance with. You can't make the excuse any more that you don't know what's going on. Sometimes it means seeing shocking things, and it's very hard to look, like the pictures from Ethiopia of those tiny starving children, covered with flies, and you wonder: however could we have let this happen?

Songs of Praise and **Praise Be!** are an important witness to our own way of life here in Britain. People all round the world, in New Zealand, Australia, the United States and Canada, in France, Holland, Belgium and Germany, can see that there are millions of us here, up and down our country, who believe in God, and who come together in our beautiful churches to sing about our faith.

Will Your Anchor Hold

As I've said, I went back to Morecambe to present **Songs of Praise** a few years ago. We were accompanied by the local Sally Army band with their conductor, which was great. And there was also a conductor for us, in the congregation, so there were two conductors, do you follow? One of the hymns we sang that night was one of my great favourites, because it always reminds me of all the Morecambe fishermen: "Will Your Anchor Hold?"

Right then. The Salvation Army Band leader raises his baton, our conductor raises his baton, and suddenly the band's away like an express train: Diddle-do-dum-dum-diddle-do-dum-dum!!! – getting to the end of the first verse and chorus in about twenty seconds flat! "Our" conductor, his hands still poised gracefully in the air, turned very slowly round and looked at them.

The Sally Army band stopped, and their conductor turned round, too, as though he was very surprised to find that none of us were singing! It was quite a little comedy routine.

We did all get together in the end, but even when the Band went at half-speed, it can't ever have been sung so fast!

Will your anchor hold in the storms of life,
When the clouds unfold their wings of strife?
When the strong tides lift, and the cables strain,
Will your anchor drift, or firm remain?

Chorus:
We have an anchor that keeps the soul
Steadfast and sure while the billows roll:
Fastened to the Rock which cannot move,
Grounded firm and deep in the Saviour's love!

Will your anchor hold in the straits of fear?
When the breakers roar and the reef is near;
While the surges rave, and the wild winds blow,
Shall the angry waves then your bark o'erflow?

Will your anchor hold in the floods of death
When the waters cold chill your latest breath?
On the rising tide you can never fail,
While your anchor holds within the veil.

Will your eyes behold through the morning light
The city of gold and the harbour bright?
Will you anchor safe by the heavenly shore,
When life's storms are past for evermore?

                              Priscilla Jane Owens (1829–1899)

Weeding and Old Wives' Tales

Scotty and I both love gardening when we're down at
our cottage in Sussex. And I have to say, though I know
I shouldn't, that on a spring or summer's day – it does
look a little picture!

We were helped a lot at the beginning by the wit and
wisdom of two ladies called Maureen and Bridget Boland,
who wrote a wonderful little book called *The Old Wives'
Lore for Gardeners*. Now you might think that in this
modern age of fertilisers and insecticides and all the
wonders of modern science that are available to us, a
collection of Old Wives' tales wouldn't be of much use.
But I'm here to tell you, I follow their advice to the letter,
and we hardly bother with any of your modern chemistry
sets.

As recommended, I plant a clove of garlic under each
of my (excuse me while I give a modest cough here!)
"Thora Hird" rose bushes, and that keeps away the

greenfly. We put a bean plant between each gooseberry bush, to keep the fruit fly off – and it works! Jan watched us doing this from a distance for quite a while, until her curiosity got the better of her, and she came over to us saying "Er, excuse me, . . .?" But it's all wonderful advice this – I should charge you, really! Did you know that if you hang mothballs on your peach tree you'll get no more leaf curl? I mean your peach tree will get no more leaf curl! The only thing Scotty drew the line at was where it advised us to sow certain seeds "only when the moon is full, and naked!"

I like a good sing when I'm gardening, and as we're right in the middle of the country I'm not afraid of upsetting anybody. (Well, you haven't heard me sing!) One day I was out there digging, and singing away, "What a friend we have in Je-e-e-sus . . ." when I got the feeling I was being watched.

I straightened up, and there, about a foot away, staring at me over the fence, with huge eyes and rather thoughtful expressions, were some cows. They were all chewing on their cuds *in time* to my singing! I stopped singing – and they all instantly stopped chewing their cuds and stood like statues! I started again – and so did they! I asked a farmer friend whether cows could be musical, and he said, "Oh, they're very nosy animals, are cows. They'd probably just come over to see what all the noise was about!"

What a Friend we have in Jesus

What a friend we have in Jesus,
All our sins and griefs to bear!
What a privilege to carry
Everything to God in prayer!
O what peace we often forfeit,
O what needless pain we bear
All because we do not carry
Everything to God in prayer!

Have we trials and temptations?
Is there trouble anywhere?
We should never be discouraged:
Take it to the Lord in prayer.
Can we find a friend so faithful,
Who will all our sorrows share?
Jesus knows our every weakness –
Take it to the Lord in prayer.

Are we weak and heavy-laden,
Cumbered with a load of care?
Jesus only is our refuge,
Take it to the Lord in prayer.
Do thy friends despise, forsake thee?
Take it to the Lord in prayer.
In His arms He'll take and shield thee,
Thou wilt find a solace there.

Joseph Scriven (1819–1886)

Xmas

Xmas without Christ
Is just a Blank Holiday.

And that's all you're getting from me under X!

Jesus said, "Have you understood all these things?"
"Yes", they replied!

(Well nothing beats having a bit of self-confidence!)

Yes!

It's nice when you can say "Yes" to people. We've all met Mr or Mrs "No". It doesn't matter what you ask them, the answer is always the same: "No. Sorry." Now, you're never like that are you? Nor me. (Not much!)

Oh dear! Just when I'm sitting comfortably, and have got everything planned in my mind for a cosy introduction to one of our favourite hymns, the **Praise Be!** Director will come over to me, all apologetic (because you couldn't have a more charming director than Valetta Stallabrass), and she'll say "Thora, I'm awfully sorry, I hope you don't mind, but we're not going to have that hymn now after all. We want to go out in the garden and film you talking to the dogs . . . ."

Now, I'm always delighted to go out and talk to Jan's dogs, Patch and Tess, but doing it for **Praise Be!** means changing all my clothes, putting on a hat (flattening my hair and spoiling it for when we come back in again), getting cold while they all change their minds at least six times about how they want to film me, and waiting for the dogs to settle down, because they get very excited with all the strange television people around, and don't want to sit still. The last thing in the world I want to do is say "Yes"! But if I didn't, a lot of very charming moments would be missed by the **Praise Be!** viewers.

Do you remember a little story I read once on **Praise Be!** about four people called Anybody, Everybody, Somebody and Nobody?

"There was an important job to be done. Anybody could have done it, and Everybody agreed that Somebody should do it, but Nobody said Yes, they would do it, so in the end Nobody did it!"

And, when you come to think of it, the whole Christian Church was built on the foundation of Mary saying "Yes" to God.

Yea, Lord we Greet Thee

Yea, Lord, we greet Thee,
Born this happy morning;
Jesu, to Thee be glory given:
Word of the Father,
Now in flesh appearing:
O come, let us adore him, O come, let us adore Him,
O come, let us adore Him, Christ the Lord!

Tr. F. Oakeley, W. T. Brooke and others

The Christian Year

The viewers choose the hymns for **Praise Be!**; but which hymn goes into which programme and in what order, is decided by a little **Praise Be!** committee of people from the **Songs of Praise** production team.

Usually the hymns chosen more or less make the decisions for us, and certain themes, like love, and Remembrance, come up again and again. Sometimes, and it's rather nice when it happens, a group of hymns between them tell the story of Jesus' journey through life, as reflected in the Church's year.

You begin at Advent, in December, with four weeks' preparation for Jesus' coming, and we sing all those wonderful Advent carols like "O Come, O Come Emmanuel", and "Lo! he comes with clouds descending", and "On Jordan's Bank the Baptist's cry".

Then everyone celebrates Christmas, Jesus' birthday, and lots of people come to church who never come at any other time, because there's something about it that still gets to them, even in these commercial, cynical days. Funnily enough, though, whenever I play some of the carols that everyone so much enjoyed singing at Christmas, on **Praise Be!** in May or June, some people will always write to me and complain! I've never understood why, but I try to remember to warn people when there's a Christmas carol coming up, so those people can go and put the kettle on!

In January rather fewer of us are left in church for Epiphany Sunday, to welcome the Three Wise Men, and celebrate the light that Jesus brought into our dark world. But we sing with a good heart: "Brightest and best of the sons of the morning", and "O worship the Lord in the beauty of holiness", and "Hills of the north rejoice!" (They don't know what they're missing, do they?)

In early spring, we think about when Jesus, straight after His baptism in the River Jordan by John the Baptist, spent forty days in the wildnerness, where He met the Devil, and defeated him, and prepared Himself for His life of teaching and healing, and for His death. This is during the six and a half weeks of Lent, and we have to think about our own lives, too, so as well as giving up chocolate and swearing, we sing "Forty days and forty nights", "Christian, dost thou see them", and "Just as I am".

On Palm Sunday we remember Jesus' last journey into Jerusalem, riding a little donkey; so we sing "Ride on, Ride on in Majesty", and "Little Donkey, carry Jesus", and "My Song is Love unknown".

Then it's Holy Week: on Maundy Thursday we remember the Last Supper, in an upper room, where Jesus washed the feet of His twelve friends, and told them to remember Him whenever they broke bread and drank wine, but one of them, Judas Iscariot, betrayed Him. After supper, they went out, singing hymns together, to the garden of Gethsemane. Jesus prayed, but the disciples fell asleep, and there He was arrested and taken away for trial for blasphemy, followed by His crucifixion on Good Friday. We sing "When I survey the wondrous Cross", and "There is a green hill far away", and "O Sacred Head".

The third day after Good Friday is the most important day of all, Easter Sunday, when Jesus rose from the dead.

Some of the greatest hymns ever written are sung on Easter day.

Ye Choirs of New Jerusalem

Ye choirs of new Jerusalem,
Your sweetest notes employ,
The Paschal victory to hymn
In strains of holy joy.

For Judah's Lion burst His chains,
And crushed the serpent's head;
And brought with Him, from death's domains,
The long-imprisoned dead.

Devouring depths of hell their prey
At this command restore;
His ransomed hosts pursue their way
Where Jesus goes before.

Triumphant in His glory now
To Him all power is given;
To Him in one communion bow
All saints in earth and heaven.

While joyful thus His praise we sing,
His mercy we implore,
Into His palace bright to bring
And keep us evermore.

All glory to the Father be,
All glory to the Son,
All glory, Holy Ghost, to Thee,
While endless ages run.

St Fulbert of Chartres
Tr. R. Campbell

Zacchaeus

Did you think I'd be caught out by Z? Not an old hand like me!

There are lots of interesting characters in the Bible whose names begin with Z: Zacharias, the priest and father of John the Baptist; Zebedee, the father of James and John, two of Jesus' disciples; and Zadok the priest in the Old Testament – don't you remember how the choir in Westminster Abbey roared out the anthem at our Queen's Coronation:

> "ZADOK, THE PRIEST AND NATHAN, THE PROPHET
> ANOINTED SOLOMON KING!'

Tremendous!

But far and away my favourite Z is the poor little rich man, Zacchaeus, whom St Luke wrote about. St Luke seems to have made a special point of telling stories about people whom nobody liked, but who became "goodies" in the end.

Jesus entered Jericho and was passing through. A man was there by the name of Zacchaeus; he was a chief tax collector and was wealthy. He wanted to see who Jesus was, but being a short man, he could not, because of the crowd. So he ran ahead and climbed a sycamore-fig tree to see Him, since Jesus was coming that way.

When Jesus reached the spot, He looked up and said to him, "Zacchaeus, come down immediately. I must stay at your house today." So he came down at once and welcomed Him gladly.

All the people saw this and began to mutter, "He has gone to be the guest of a 'sinner'."

But Zacchaeus stood up and said to the Lord, "Look, Lord! Here and now I give half of my possessions to the poor, and if I have cheated anybody out of anything, I will pay back four times the amount."

Jesus said to him, "Today salvation has come to this house, because this man, too, is a son of Abraham. For the Son of Man came to seek and to save what was lost."

Luke 19: 1–9 (NIV)

In the gospels it is taken for granted that if you are rich you must be a sinner. But good old Zacchaeus said "Yes" to Jesus, who knew from the start that no one who climbed up into a sycamore fig tree to look at Him could be all bad!

Zion

I've not finished with the Zs yet! Zion is the name of the hill on which Jerusalem was built, and came by association to mean the holy city itself, particularly the ideal Jerusalem of the future, where God would make His home on earth and to which all nations would come and worship Him.

For devout Jews, the words of Psalm 137 express the strength of their feelings about Zion, written when they were in Exile in Babylon.

By the waters of Babylon there we sat down, yea, we wept, when we remembered Zion.

We hanged our harps upon the willows in the midst
thereof.
For there they that carried us away captive required of
us a song; and they that wasted us required of us mirth,
saying, "Sing us one of the songs of Zion".
How shall we sing the Lord's song in a strange land?

Psalm 137:1–4 (AV)

Christians have adopted Zion as their name for the City
of God in heaven. No words more poetically express our
idea of Zion than John Newton's hymn "Glorious things
of thee are spoken".

I remember talking to Canon Cyril Taylor on **Praise Be!**
a few years ago, who composed the beautiful tune
Abbot's Leigh, which has almost supplanted Haydn's
Austrian National Anthem as the music we most often
sing it to. Canon Taylor demonstrated to me how, when
he was conducting his own choir, he would duck down
out of sight on the third last note of the last line of each
verse, in order to make them sing it low enough,
otherwise they sang it a third too high! I wondered where
on earth he had gone!

Glorious Things of Thee are Spoken

> Glorious things of thee are spoken,
> Zion, city of our God!
> He whose word cannot be broken
> Formed thee for his own abode:
> On the Rock of Ages founded,
> What can shake thy sure repose?

With salvation's walls surrounded,
Thou may'st smile at all thy foes.

See, the streams of living waters,
Springing from eternal love,
Well supply thy sons and daughters,
And all fear of want remove:
Who can faint while such a river
Ever flows their thirst to assuage?
Grace, which like the Lord the Giver,
Never fails from age to age.

Saviour, if of Zion's city
I, through grace, a member am,
Let the world deride or pity,
I will glory in Thy name:
Fading is the worldling's pleasure,
All his boasted pomp and show;
Solid joys and lasting treasure
None but Zion's children know.

John Newton (1725–1807)

Zoom in!

If you were ever to come across a production script for
Praise Be!, you would find against the closing item of the
last programme the words: ZOOM IN TO BCU THORA.
Now what can that mean? Well, I'll tell you.

I always feel a bit emotional when the time comes to
say goodbye to the viewers at the end of each series. I've
had fourteen very happy years presenting **Praise Be!** but
each year you can never be sure that there will be another

one. The powers that be at the BBC might decide any day "O, we've had enough of **Praise Be!**, let's do something else instead." Or even, "O, we've had enough of Thora. Let's find someone new." So at the end of every series, I always think it might really be goodbye for the last time, and so I feel a little sad, although because of this ZOOM IN TO BCU THORA business, I try very hard not to show it! Yes, I'm just about to explain.

You see, the naughty director knows that I may be going to get a bit choked up, so she instructs the cameraperson to ZOOM IN TO BCU THORA, meaning she wants to fill your television screen with a Big Close Up of Thora's poor sad face! She thinks the viewers are cruel people, who enjoy watching others in distress! No, no, not really! Valetta knows that many of the viewers are sad, because they are kind enough to sincerely miss me when I go, and she wants them to know that I will miss them too.

I always remind myself, and the viewers, that although **Praise Be!** may be coming to an end for another year, a new series of **Songs of Praise** is just beginning, with visits to more chapels, churches and cathedrals all over the country, and more choirs and congregations coming together to sing all our favourite hymns, and to introduce us to many new ones, some of which will perhaps become tomorrow's "old favourites".

And now it's time to end this book, but not on a sad note. I wonder how many of you remember a little girl called Katy, who appeared on **Songs of Praise** from Grantham, quite a few years ago now. Katy was eight or nine and had been born with Spina Bifida, and I think she had just won a brownie award for bravery. She talked to Gerry Monte about her swimming, and riding, and how her favourite pony was called Star. She was the tiniest little thing, with shining eyes full of happiness, and what she mostly said, in her shy, breathless voice was "Yes!" We saw her on **Praise Be!** and the hymn she chose is the one I'd like to end this book on, "Glad that I live am I". It's people like Katy and her shining eyes which make **Songs of Praise** so many people's favourite programme.

Glad that I Live Am I

Glad that I live am I
That the sky is blue,
Glad for the country lanes
And the fall of dew.

After the sun the rain,
After the rain the sun,
This is the way of life
Till the work be done.

All that we need to do
Be we low or high
Is to see that we grow
Nearer the sky.

Lizette Woodworth Reese
(1856–1935)

Deep Peace

Goodbye and God bless you, and, in the words of the old Gaelic blessing:

> Deep peace of the running wave
> to you,
> Deep peace of the flowing air
> to you,
> Deep peace of the quiet earth
> to you,
> Deep peace of the shining stars
> to you,
> Deep peace of the watching shepherds
> to you,
> Deep peace of the Son of Peace
> to you.